What Others Are Saying About
Youth Ministry from the Inside Out

"I so appreciate Mike Higgs's honesty, integrity and biblical insights in addressing such a needed perspective on youth ministry. He writes from a wealth of experience and expertise!"

NANCY WILSON, ASSOCIATE NATIONAL DIRECTOR, STUDENT VENTURE

"I know of no one of national stature better qualified to write on keys to the renewal of youth ministry in America than Mike Higgs. I've worked side by side with him in major youth events. I've seen his heart for Christ, for young people and, at a profound level, for others in ministry to Christian young people. Now you can get close to Mike's heart too. This is not a book of how-tos for youth ministry. This is a book on how to *be* Christ-empowered youth ministers."

DAVID BRYANT, CHAIRMAN, AMERICA'S NATIONAL PRAYER COMMITTEE, FOUNDER, PROCLAIM HOPE!

"As I read this book I remembered why I was drawn to Mike Higgs ten years go. It was his spiritual honesty, his dissatisfaction with the status quo and his passionate pursuit of God. Mike, thank you for this challenge to be changed, and for inviting us to 'snorkel' with you in God's great River!"

EDDIE SMITH, FOUNDER/PRESIDENT, U.S. PRAYER CENTER

"*Youth Ministry from the Inside Out* is an apt description of what has proven so effective in Mike Higgs's life experience. Apply the principles and discover a greater depth and vitality in your daily ministry."

PAUL FLEISCHMANN, PRESIDENT, NATIONAL NETWORK OF YOUTH MINISTRIES

YOUTH MINISTRY FROM THE INSIDE OUT

How who you are shapes what you do

M I K E   H I G G S

InterVarsity Press
Downers Grove, Illinois

InterVarsity Press
P.O. Box 1400, Downers Grove, IL 60515-1426
World Wide Web: www.ivpress.com
E-mail: mail@ivpress.com

InterVarsity Press® is the book-publishing division of InterVarsity Christian Fellowship/USA®, a student movement active on campus at hundreds of universities, colleges and schools of nursing in the United States of America, and a member movement of the International Fellowship of Evangelical Students. For information about local and regional activities, write Public Relations Dept., InterVarsity Christian Fellowship/USA, 6400 Schroeder Rd., P.O. Box 7895, Madison, WI 53707-7895, or visit the IVCF website at <www.ivcf.org>.

Cover design: Cindy Kiple

Cover and interior image: Stock Image/Image State

ISBN 0-8308-2399-9

Printed in the United States of America ∞

Library of Congress Cataloging-in-Publication Data

Higgs, Mike, 1954-
   Youth ministry from the inside out: how who you are shapes what you
do / Mike Higgs.
      p. cm.
Includes bibliographical references.
   ISBN 0-8308-2399-9 (pbk.: alk paper)
 1. Church group work with youth. I. Title.
  BV4447.H48 2003
  259′.23—dc21

                                                                                                    2003006797

P	18	17	16	15	14	13	12	11	10	9	8	7	6	5	4	3	2	1
Y	18	17	16	15	14	13	12	11	10	09	08	07	06	05	04	03		

To my bride and soulmate, Terri,

Who lives from the inside out

And is teaching me how to hear God's voice.

PROGRAM

T H A N K S

To my bride, Terri: you believe in me much more than I do. Without you, this book wouldn't be happening. And our adventure is just beginning. Bolo love.

To my children, Lilly and Levi: thanks in part to you two, I am able to write from a place of joy (and craziness) at home.

To H. D. and Loce: David had one Jonathan, while I have had two for over a quarter-century. This book is the result of decades of your prodding during our annual fishing expeditions. May we all get "freight-trained" next time out!

To my board—Mac, Glu, Prof, Fish, Doc, Howdy: you believed in what I do even when you didn't (and perhaps still don't) understand it all.

To Ron Kincade: you were my first model of how to do relational, incarnational youth ministry. It worked on me!

To Dan Pitney: when I joined our fraternity, the last thing on my mind was that it would be a place where someone would disciple me. It was; you did.

To Gary Casady: you paved the way for my career switch from journalist to youth pastor, tolerated my immature arrogance for far too long and nurtured the seeds of ministry in me even when they threatened to grow into weeds.

To Cindy Bunch and Dave Zimmerman at IVP: your wisdom and help have been invaluable. You are both "the bomb" at what you do; I just hope you know what you are getting into!

To my Lord Jesus: I now know you are more concerned about who I am to you than what I do for you.

THE YOUTH MINISTRY
SYMPHONY
An Explanation and Introduction

---

sym•pho•ny (sĭm′fə-nē)

1. An extended piece of music, for orchestra, in three or more movements.
2. A symphonic orchestra.
3. An orchestral concert.
4. Something characterized by a harmonious combination of elements.[1]

re•new (rĭ-nōo′)

1. To make new or as if new again; restore.
2. To take up again; resume.
3. To regain or restore the physical or mental vigor of; revive.
4. To replenish.
5. To bring into being again; reestablish.

A symphonic orchestra is comprised of many musicians and instruments. Although each musician can play his or her instrument well, the musicians need each other. No musician or instrument is more important than another, nor can the orchestra play the symphony without every musician and every instrument. The composer wrote the symphony with every instrument in mind. The violin section cannot say, "We don't need the cellos," or the oboe section say, "We can play without the percussion." Every instrument, be it piccolo or viola or clarinet, is essential to the success of the orchestra. Only when the musicians all play together, under the direction of the conductor, can the glory of the symphony be heard.

■   ■   ■

The passage above is my own version (MOV) of 1 Corinthians 12:12-26. Paul actually uses a body metaphor in this text to describe the church; I rewrote it partly because my daughter plays the violin, so the orchestra metaphor is particularly relevant to me these days. It's also helpful to hear a fresh "spin" on a Bible passage from time to time.

The Orchestra of Youth Ministry

In my ministry travels, I get to see a variety of youth ministry philosophies, styles and programs. I find that some focus for the most part on churched kids and discipleship, while others target the unchurched and emphasize evangelism. Some do both. Some youth groups are populated with kids sporting Tommy Hilfiger and Abercrombie & Fitch gear; other groups consist of students with multiple body piercings and tattoos. Some ministries baptize by immersion; others do so by sprinkling. A few probably dry clean. But whatever their style or method, I enjoy them all. Their diversity flows out of and reflects the heart of God, the Divine Composer. As the Conductor, the Holy Spirit, works with the diverse "instruments" to get them to play together, they produce heavenly music of incomparable beauty. The orchestra of the church, under the expert baton of the Conductor, plays a symphony that is both pleasing to God and touching to the hearts of those created to hear it.

I have structured what follows with this metaphor in mind. My musical expertise is mostly limited to thrashing on the guitar as a song **leader,*** so I won't stretch the metaphor too far. But I think it is appropriate in terms of both the style and the content of what you will be reading.

> *"YOUTH WORSHIP LEADER" IS A RECENT ADDITION TO THE YOUTH MINISTRY LEXICON.

A symphony is usually comprised of three to four movements. To get the most out of the symphony it is best to listen from beginning to end. But you can, if you so choose, listen to one or more of the movements alone and still enjoy the music. Stylistically, I have divided this book into movements as well. While it is best to read it from start to finish, if you choose to skip a movement, or a chapter within a movement, that's cool; you can still benefit from the sections that you do read.

I wrote this book with every member of the youth ministry "orchestra" in mind. Although I occasionally mention youth ministry methodology and strategy, my focus is on transferable principles—biblical truths that will make us all better youth ministry "musicians" no matter what "instrument" we play, be it first chair violin or the person who gets to slam the cymbals together from time to time. I address issues that relate to individual youth worker "musicians" as well as to the youth ministry symphonic orchestra as a whole.

But be forewarned: this is not a book about how to do youth ministry. It is a book about how to be youth ministers, vocational or volunteer, both individually and corporately. The distinction, in my mind, is huge.

Being Versus Doing

We are all familiar with the story of Jesus at the home of Mary and Martha. Mary was hanging out with Jesus, while Martha was busy preparing sushi in the kitchen, more than a little bothered that she wasn't getting any help from her sister. Jesus addressed her stress: " 'Martha, Martha,' the Lord answered, 'you are worried and upset about many things, but only one thing is needed. Mary has chosen what is better, and it will not be taken away from her' " (Luke 10:41-42).

Martha was, at her core, a do-er, while Mary was more of a be-er. We see this at the funeral of their brother Lazarus, when Martha ran out to meet Jesus as he approached to ask him why he didn't show up earlier to keep their brother from dying, while Mary remained at home. One could also say that Martha operated primarily from the "outside," while Mary did so from the "inside"—if you catch my drift.

✳I WOULD HAVE MADE BLACKENED GALILEAN FISH— I HATE SUSHI.

I can identify with Martha; I would have run out to meet Jesus as well. And to be honest, I probably would have been in the **kitchen*** too. I tend to be an "outside first" guy; most youth workers are. Perhaps it is built into our DNA. We have this tendency to be more concerned about how to *do* youth ministry well than how to *be* youth ministers well. And that, according to Jesus, can be a problem.

Obviously, doing is not a bad thing. Without Martha, Jesus and Mary would have gone hungry. Mary wasn't all right and Martha all wrong. Similarly, both an inside and outside approach are needed for effective ministry. The problem is the tendency of youth ministry, and many youth workers, to have an imbalanced emphasis on the outside of youth ministry—how we do it—and a corresponding neglect of the inside, or being—who we are as youth workers. The outside of youth ministry needs to flow from the inside of youth workers. Given the current state of much of youth ministry, one might even say that youth ministry needs to be turned inside out.

I have been doing youth ministry for a quarter century and have no plans to take a demotion to any other line of work. I love youth, I love youth workers, I love youth ministry, and I think I'm wired for it—I think young, **act young*** and feel young. Only my birth certificate and my mirror betray me. But a fair amount of individual and corporate fine tuning is in order if we are to play the Divine Symphony that will reach the emerging generations of youth. Yes, it will take a thorough understanding of postmodernism; yes, we will always need to be culturally aware and relevant in our style and message. But we have not even come close to seeing the Great Commission fulfilled among recent generations of young people (at least in Western countries), and the prognosis for the future is not encouraging if the research of folks like George Barna is right. In his 1999 report "Third Millennium Teens," Barna identifies myths and realities of the state of youth ministry:

*ON OCCASION I ACT TOO YOUNG, SAY MY DAUGHTER AND SON.

Myth:　The church is where teen spiritual progress is made.

Reality:　Spiritual development in teenagers depends mostly on their family.

Myth: Today's youth group attenders are tomorrow's church leaders.

Reality: Today's youth group attenders are tomorrow's unchurched.

Barna summarizes: "If we continue to minister in ways in which we are doing so today, we are strategically facilitating the demise of the Church we exist to build."[2]

Turning youth ministry inside out could also be called youth ministry renewal. The dictionary defines *renewal* using a whole lot of other "re-" verbs—*restore, resume, regain, revive, replenish, reestablish*—each of which is a part of spiritual renewal. The prefix *re* implies going back to something that was previously attained or returning to an earlier state. I like that.

*LET'S KEEP THE WATER BALLOON SLINGSHOTS— THEY'RE STILL FRESH.

Let me clarify, though: I have no desire to go back to the days of youth ministry when I spent Wednesday afternoons reinforcing cardboard refrigerator boxes with duct tape so they wouldn't explode when kids slammed into each other with the boxes over their heads. Or once again wiring a wire mesh-seated stool with a sizable battery to make the infamous "hot seat." **No thank you.** * And "Kumbaya," "One in the Spirit" and "Pass It On" are probably best left in the annals of youth ministry hymnology.

By using the word *renewal* in reference to inside-out youth ministry, I am alluding to a variety of spiritual "going backs":

- going back to our first love
- going back to the time when we were more excited about being followers of Jesus than we were about doing ministry

- going back to a fresh Isaiah-style encounter with the Living God that both ruins us and heals us
- going back to the place of prayer, which includes both talking to God and slowing down enough to hear his still small voice
- going back to the time when we were more desperate to see kids ushered into the kingdom than we were to look good attempting it
- going back to a relational, incarnational approach to ministry with an emphasis on the latter characteristic
- going back to the words of Jesus and realizing that love and unity are a really big deal to God

This is the flavor of inside-out renewal that will fill the pages to come. When we youth ministry musicians are playing our instruments together, under the direction of the Conductor, the Composer will be honored and glorified as his divine music reverberates throughout all creation. We will reach generations of youth, and his kingdom will advance in radical and wonderful ways.

Restore us to yourself, O LORD, that we may return;
   renew our days as of old. (Lamentations 5:21)

SELAH

Come, Thou Almighty King, help us Thy name to sing,
*   help us to praise.*
Father, all-glorious, o'er all victorious,
Come, and reign over us, Ancient of Days.

Come, Thou Incarnate Word, gird on Thy mighty
*   sword, our prayer attend:*
Come, and Thy people bless, and give Thy Word
*   success;*
* Spirit of holiness, on us descend.*

Come, Holy Comforter, Thy sacred witness bear in this
*   glad hour:*
Thou who almighty art, now rule in every heart,
* And ne'er from us depart, Spirit of power.*

To Thee, great One in Three, eternal praises be hence
*   evermore.*
Thy sovereign majesty may we in glory see,
And to eternity love and adore.

"COME, THOU ALMIGHTY KING"
ANONYMOUS, CIRCA 1757

FIRST MOVEMENT

RENEWING YOUR SELF

"I AM DESPERATE"

An Embracing of Brokenness

---

des•per•ate (děs′pər-ĭt)

1. Marked by, arising from, or showing despair.
2. Undertaken out of extreme urgency or as a last resort.
3. Nearly hopeless; critical.
4. Suffering or driven by great need or distress.

My dad grew up in southeastern Oregon, a vast expanse of desert and sagebrush punctuated with the occasional ranch and even more occasional community. It was a culture where actions spoke much louder than words, and substance was preferred over style. Even after he was over a half century removed from that environment, Dad occasionally reverted to rancher jargon in describing someone whose assets or accomplishments didn't back up his boastful speech or appearance of affluence: "Big hat, no cattle."

In recent years the Western church has come under considerable scrutiny and criticism for a similar malady: we have "big hats" of style but sometimes are lacking in the "cattle" of substance. Over the past few decades, we have published millions of Christian books, burned millions of Christian music CDs, sold many millions of dollars worth of Christian T-shirts, pencils, bumper stickers and assorted other paraphernalia, and logged uncountable hours of radio and TV broadcasts. Yet we have done far too little to stem the moral and ethical decay of our country, much less advance the kingdom of God in significant ways.

Although youth ministry has been a vanguard of trends such as networking and strategic collaboration, we would be dishonest not to admit that the "big hat, no cattle" tag applies to us more than we would like. Yes, youth ministry has certainly come of age over the past few decades. We are generally biblically and philosophically sound and culturally relevant. We understand the importance of campus ministry and the best ways to make it happen. We tend to value relational ministry and understand how to present the gospel to teenagers in a relevant manner. We often see students come to Christ. We make disciples. We work with increasing effectiveness with parents and families. We are "professional." And we are doing a pretty good job. But unless the statistics lie, we still have quite a ways to go to fulfill the Great Commission among students.

Contemporary youth ministry has at its disposal more training materials, books, Sunday school curricula, conferences and various other resources than at any time in history. So how come we haven't made a more significant impact in the youth culture we seek to reach? Postmodern author Leonard Sweet is blunt but honest:

> Traditional "youth ministry" won't work any longer. Nor does the entertainment/message model of the 60's and 70's. Nor does the "trickle-down" strategy . . . in which you attract the most popular kids, the "group" that is "in," and you've got everyone else. Why?
>
> No one "group" is "in" anymore; groups have demassified into affinity communities. There is no one "youth ministry" possible anymore because there is now not

one "youth group" anymore. Besides the jocks, there are now the bands, blacks, blonds, brains, computer people, cools, crews, ·dorks, druggies, floaters, FOBs (fresh off the boat), friendlies, groovies, hippies, losers, nerds, nobodies, normals, overly violent, . . . partiers, peace freaks, pom-poms, rappers, richies, . . . smokers, snobs, stoners, tides, trendies, wannabes, wavers, weirdos, and yuppies."[1]

Mark Senter concurs with Sweet:

The decade . . . has drawn to a close and the health of ministries to high school students in the United States is less than exciting. . . . The time has come for revolution—a total restructuring of youth ministry. Continued modifications of the current system simply will not keep up with the changes in the world in which we live. . . . There is no way in which the tactics currently being used will stem the tidal wave of spiritual, moral, and psychological problems faced by the current and coming generations of adolescents.[2]

Clearly, something has to change in order for us to minister effectively to youth. But what is that something?

A Response Born of Desperation

When Jehoshaphat, king of Judah, discovered that invading armies were at his doorstep (2 Chronicles 20:1-3), his normal response would have been to sound the *shofar** and muster his army as quickly as possible to defend the city. That was the standard operating procedure in a country familiar with invading armies and

**TRANSLATION:
BUGLE.**

the tactics of warfare. But Jehoshaphat didn't respond normally. The invading armies were too big (the Bible says they
were "vast") and too close (Hazazon Tamar, or En Gedi, was a
small oasis on the west coast of the Dead Sea about twenty-five
miles away; access to Jerusalem was only by narrow paths up
the steep cliffs from the shore, so it was not a common attack
route, thus the surprise). He realized that despite the reputa-
tion of the army of Judah as valiant warriors, this particular
battle had defeat written all over it.

So Jehoshaphat responded by calling his people together
not to prepare for battle but to pray and fast. In verses 6-12 he
leads his people in a heart-felt prayer that acknowledges
God's sovereignty (v. 6) and past faithfulness (vv. 7-9). But it is
the end of his prayer that reveals his heart: "O our God, will
you not judge them? For we have no power to face this vast
army that is attacking us. *We do not know what to do, but our eyes
are upon you*" (2 Chronicles 20:12, emphasis mine).

Jehoshaphat was a true biblical realist. He saw his circumstances as they really were and humbly admitted that his army,
on its own, had no chance of victory. He also admitted that as a
seasoned military commander in charge of veteran troops, he
had no clue what to do to divert disaster. So he chose to shift his
focus and that of his countrymen from the opposing armies and
the battle itself to God and God alone. They fixed their eyes
firmly on the only Source of both victory and the power to accomplish it. In doing so, he came to see his circumstances from
God's perspective. He recognized that their obstacle was God's
opportunity.

God responded to Jehoshaphat's humble prayer of desperation with a prophetic word of encouragement from Jahaziel
(2 Chronicles 20:14-17), as well as a battle strategy unlike any
they had utilized before: they were to place at the front of the

army not the shield-bearers or spear-throwers or archers, but the worship leaders! The Chronicler records the result:

> After consulting the people, Jehoshaphat appointed men to sing to the LORD and to praise him for the splendor of his holiness as they went out at the head of the army, saying:
>
>> "Give thanks to the LORD,
>> for his love endures forever."
>
> As they began to sing and praise, the LORD set ambushes against the men of Ammon and Moab and Mount Seir who were invading Judah, and they were defeated. (2 Chronicles 20:21-22)

Jehoshaphat's example is foundational in our discussion of youth ministry from the inside out. He turned to God in humility and desperation because he didn't have another option. As youth workers engaged in an epic spiritual battle for the lives of emerging generations of youth, we also don't have any other options but to humbly seek God.

Youth workers must become desperate. If it's true that the emerging generations of youth are in a **desperate situation,*** and if it's true that desperate situations demand desperate measures, it's time for desperate praying and desperate ministering. Yet isn't it also true that such works of desperation are just that— works—unless they spring from an awareness of our *own* desperation and brokenness?

*DO I HEAR AN "AMEN"?

Sensing the despair of a hopeless generation may, indeed, make us desperate to bring them a message of hope. But our desperation must begin at a deeper, personal level.

Do not hold against us the sins of the fathers;
    may your mercy come quickly to meet us,
    for we are in desperate need.

Help us, O God our Savior,
    for the glory of your name;
deliver us and forgive our sins
    for your name's sake. (Psalm 79:8-9)

The sacrifices of God are a broken spirit;
    a broken and contrite heart,
    O God, you will not despise. (Psalm 51:17)

This is the one I esteem:
    he who is humble and contrite in spirit,
    and trembles at my word. (Isaiah 66:2)

Turning youth ministry inside out requires a desperation that begins in our own lives. Nancy Leigh DeMoss goes to the heart of the matter:

Before its impact can be felt in a home, a church, or a nation, revival must first be experienced on a personal level in the hearts of men and women who have encountered God in a fresh way. And the single greatest hindrance to our experiencing personal revival is our unwillingness to humble ourselves and confess our desperate need for His mercy. Our generation has been programmed to pursue happiness, wholeness, good feelings about ourselves, positive self-image, affirmation, and cures for our hurt feelings and damaged psyches. But God is not as interested in these ends as we are. He is more committed to making us holy than making us happy. And there is only one pathway to holiness—

one road to genuine revival—and that is the pathway of humility or brokenness.[3]

Tim St. Clair defines *brokenness* as "our response of humility and obedience to the conviction of God's Spirit or the revelation of God's Word, . . . the shattering of a person's will so that every response is under the control of the Holy Spirit of God."[4] Youth ministry from the inside out begins with our acknowledgment, individually and corporately, that we are broken people who tend to minister out of the "broken cisterns" (Jeremiah 2:13-14) of personal skills and charisma, tried and true programs, or creative strategies. It begins with our realization that we desperately need renewal, day by day, individually and corporately.

These are strong words, but they come from the depth of my own heart as I daily acknowledge my own brokenness and desperation. As Jesus wept over Jerusalem, I have wept over the generations of youth to which I am called. Likely you have as well. But increasingly, I weep over my own "stuff"—pride, arrogance and rebellion, feelings of self-importance, a desire for recognition and a tendency to follow my sinful nature (Romans 7:15-20).

I have been doing youth ministry long enough that I know how to say all the right words and wear the "big hat" of competency. As one who now ministers in the prayer movement, I can do the same in that realm. But I know that inside things are not always as they outwardly appear. When I taught kids in my youth groups about sin, I used to ask for volunteers to write their ten worst sins of thought or action during the past week on a transparency so I could project them on the wall for the rest of us to see. That would generate a lot of chuckles but very few volunteers. I would never want my sins projected on the wall. I am very aware that behind my supposed big hat is a very, very small herd of cattle. I need renewal. And so the cry of my own heart has increasingly echoed that of Habakkuk, who even as he pondered the promise of renewal and revival where

> the earth will be filled with the knowledge of the glory of
> > the Lord,
> > as the waters cover the sea (Habakkuk 2:14),

still cried out to God:

> LORD, I have heard of your fame;
> > I stand in awe of your deeds, O LORD.
> Renew them in our day,
> > in our time make them known;
> > in wrath remember mercy. (3:2)

Lord, have mercy on me.

T W O

"I AM RUINED"

A Call to Consecration

---

con•se•cra•tion (kŏn'sĭ-krā'shən)

The act, or state, of:
1. Declaring or setting apart someone or something as sacred.
2. Dedication solemnly to a service or goal.
3. Sanctification.

I was driving down the road, listening to a taped sermon by a well-known minister preaching at a church where I used to serve as youth pastor, when it hit me like a **gunshot.*** In the midst of his typically powerful message, he suddenly paused, then intoned, "I have a word from the Lord for you. Consecrate yourselves, for tomorrow the Lord will do amazing things among you."

Immediately I shut off the tape and broke out in a debilitating case of "goosies." Because I knew the preacher pretty well, I was aware that such a prophetic utterance was rather out of the ordinary for him (and for the church!). But I was also quite familiar with the situation at the church, so I knew he was both accurate and timely in his word. And more important, I also

*I'VE NEVER BEEN SHOT, UNLESS YOU COUNT WHEN MY BROTHER DRILLED ME IN THE BACK WITH A BB GUN.

knew that this word was accurate and timely for me as well.

The preacher's word was a literal quote from the book of Joshua (3:5), where, after forty years of a manna-sustained tromp in the desert, the Israelites were finally ready to enter and possess their inheritance. Joshua had just taken the reins of leadership from the recently deceased Moses. Since he was one of the original twelve spies who had scouted out the land decades ago, Joshua knew where they were headed and what they faced. And he wasn't interested in another sin-induced detour. So as the nation prepared to cross the Jordan River and actually set foot on their promised inheritance, Joshua exhorted the people to consecrate themselves.

The *NIV Compact Dictionary* defines *consecration* as "an act by which a person or thing is dedicated to the service and worship of God."[1] This practice of dedicating people and things to God as an act of worship was not an unfamiliar concept to the Israelites. A significant chunk of the Mosaic law had to do with the consecration of priests, of items used in the tabernacle and of the people in general: "Consecrate yourselves and be holy, because I am the LORD your God. Keep my decrees and follow them. I am the LORD, who makes you holy" (Leviticus 20:7-8). Consecration was mandatory for a holy God to dwell among his sinful people and successfully lead them to possess their inheritance.

The Israelites' forty-year Mannafest in the desert was due in part to the fact that consecration, along with its sibling, obedience (note Leviticus 20:8), had not been taken seriously. This time around, Joshua was insistent that they take consecration *very* seriously. He knew that their success in driving out the resident "-ites"—Canaanites, Hittites, Hivites, Perizzites, Girgashites, Termites and so on—would depend entirely on their obedience. Their consecration was a declaration, in word and deed, of their obedient intentions.

Like the Israelites, we who serve in youth ministry must obediently heed Joshua's call to consecration. Far too many of us have been *sidelined* or *flatlined* in ministry, and as a result we have ended up wandering in the desert rather than claiming our inheritance as God's children. Instead, we need to be *streamlined* into lean, mean obedience machines. Only through obedience will we receive the full measure of our inheritance—joyful fulfillment and radical advancement of the kingdom among emerging generations of youth. By making a commitment to holiness, we put ourselves in a position to be filled with God's presence and power for service in his kingdom.

Sidelined or Flatlined

I recall two incidents (there were probably more) when I, a fullback on my high school football team, was relegated from the backfield to the bench. One time the play had me going right but I went left; our quarterback got pancaked. Another time a battering ram of a defensive end hit me so hard, and so many times, that I resorted to "olé" blocking—the kind of blocking a matador does when a bull comes at him. On both occasions my coach was quick to yank me off the field and let me simmer on the sidelines.

Similarly (work with me on the comparison here) more than a few youth workers are taken out of the game prematurely. Some are *sidelined* by moral default or a potential fatal flaw that progressed from a tiny crack to a gaping chasm of character. And some are *flatlined*, falling victim to the dreaded "youth ministry burnout." Sadly, the longer you are in youth ministry, the longer your list of sidelined and flatlined comrades becomes. And the obvious question is *Why?*

What are the issues that took them out of action much too soon?

I can say from personal experience there are no simple answers. But if there is a common thread that connects many of our sidelined and flatlined brothers and sisters, it is this: their view of God and of themselves has become **distorted,*** to the point that it has taken them out of the game. If you are reading this, chances are you're still on the playing field. But that doesn't mean that a distortion isn't festering inside in some way, depriving you of all Christ has in store for you, robbing you of your joy, making ministry a chore rather than a privilege.

*HANG IN THERE AS I DEVELOP THIS CONCEPT OF DISTORTION.

To put it **simply,*** personal renewal begins with discovering—or rediscovering—God's holiness. For it is in the light of God's holiness that we see how messed up we are in comparison to him and how desperately we need his forgiveness, cleansing and empowerment for Christian living and ministry. And when we are absolutely convinced that we can't do anything worthwhile on our own, but that we can "do everything through [Christ] who strengthens [us]" (Philippians 4:13), then we are renewed, or revived, and new power erupts in our lives and ministries.

*THIS CERTAINLY ISN'T SIMPLE; FOLKS WRITE MULTIPLE VOLUMES ON THIS STUFF.

That's pretty much what happened to Isaiah. He got a firsthand look at the holiness of God, and as a result, he saw himself as he really was—flawed, sinful and unclean. And his **response*** was predictable: "'Woe is me!' I cried. 'I am ruined! For I am a man of unclean lips, and I live among a people of unclean lips, and my eyes have seen the King, the LORD Almighty' " (Isaiah 6:5). When the character of the Living God was revealed to him, Isaiah realized more clearly than ever before what he was

*I WOULD HAVE FREAKED BIG-TIME.

really like—not what he thought he should be like, or what he would want to be like, but the cold, harsh truth. And it was not pretty.

Our response should be the same as Isaiah's. Joe Aldrich reminds us, "True revival begins with the acknowledgment that Isaiah is right; we are a people of unclean lips."[2] The late Dave Busby, a rare prophetic voice in youth ministry, concurred: "We can never overestimate our need for forgiveness. [Yet] if forgiveness is to mean anything we first must see our need. God's grace does not mean a thing if we don't see that we need it."[3]

Most of us are not going to have an Isaiahlike experience, but we all can discover—or rediscover—God's holiness in a way that sets our own humanity and wretchedness in stark contrast. Seeing the chasm between God's character and our own is, as Aldrich notes above, the first step to revival.

Busby, whose messages paved the way for the embers of renewal and revival we now see smoldering in many venues, gives an excellent outline of the progression necessary for personal renewal to begin. He writes:

The first step is tasting my personal depravity ("Cheer up, you're worse off than you think.") God can use this deep taste of my daily battle with indwelling sin to:

> —Break me—"The sacrifices of God are a broken spirit; a broken and contrite heart, O God, you will not despise." (Ps. 51:17)
> —Free me—from self-improvement strategies, to casting myself on God's sufficient grace.
> —Humble me—God gives grace to the humble.
> —"Gentle" me—I deal gently with others when I see my own stuff (Heb. 5:2).

Yet when I taste my personal depravity, I can devise wrong strategies to deal with it, such as:

> —Deny, hide, or pretend (as in Adam and Eve).
> —Blame others (as in Adam).
> —Self-improvement (try harder to be a better Christian).
> —Self-condemnation (shaming and indicting myself).

Or, when I taste my own personal depravity, I can also taste Calvary. ("Cheer up, you're better off than you thought.") I can:

> —Realize that there is nothing I can do to ever redeem myself or perform my way out of my sinfulness.
> —Realize that Calvary fully absorbs my depravity, that I am forgiven for Jesus' sake, that He died for ME.
> —Stay at the Cross until I "hear" the unbelievable words, "you are forgiven . . . don't bother me with this anymore . . . go on out and play."
> —Be assured, by the grace of Calvary, of daily grace that empowers me by faith to obey (Rom. 8:32).[4]

The distortions in our lives often have their source in our failure to acknowledge how messed up we are apart from Christ. Those distortions can lead us to wrong strategies for dealing with our depravity, some of which Busby mentions above. Most of us have **tried*** one or more of them. Eventually our misperceptions, if left untreated, will lead to a fruitless, frustrating personal life and ministry or take us out of youth work altogether.

*COME ON, ADMIT IT: YOU'VE TRIED AT LEAST ONE.

Please understand we all are going to have to deal with our depravity at some point. We can do so by discovering, or rediscovering, God's holiness and our own "unclean lips," realizing how ruined we are apart from him. Or we can allow the junk to build up slowly on its own in our attitudes and actions and through our ineffective strategies to deal with it. If we follow the latter path, then we will either be sidelined from vocational ministry by moral or ethical fault, or be spiritually and emotionally flatlined until we are just going through the motions of ministry (and sometimes of living). The sooner we acknowledge the junk in our lives, the sooner we can embrace the cross and the fact that no matter how **messed up*** we are, Jesus died so that the entire mess might be put to death with him, "in order that, just as Christ was raised from the dead through the glory of the Father, we too may live a new life" (Romans 6:4).

*WE ARE ALL MESSED UP.

Several years ago I ran out of gas physically and spiritually—to the extent that I had to bail out of local church youth pastoring—because I had let the junk in my life build up. I had spent a lifetime of ministry devising ineffective strategies to deal with my depravity, and I hadn't even realized it. I was a pedal-to-the-metal kind of youth worker, high on energy and enthusiasm, and willing to push myself as hard as necessary to create a successful ministry and thus validate myself (so I thought). My ministry had its ups and downs, so my level of validation rose and fell accordingly. But when I woke up one morning to find that my pedal would no longer go to the metal, my means of validation was gone. My misperceptions (and depravity) revealed, I then painfully learned the wonderfully freeing truth that a holy God loves me and died for me exactly the way that I am (junk and all), and that he is infinitely more concerned about who I am to him than what I do for him (more on that later).

So what does this have to do with calling youth workers to consecration? Pretty much everything. Remember that Isaiah received his prophetic commissioning after his "I am ruined!" experience. He rediscovered God's holiness, saw his own depravity, received forgiveness and then was fired up for some serious kingdom work! Similarly, when we admit to ourselves and to God how messed up we are in comparison to God's holiness, then we can begin the process of abandoning the distortions and strategies that we have devised in order to ignore our depravity. Daily (actually, moment by moment) choosing to embrace the cross and rely on the grace of God and the power of the Holy Spirit enables us to live victorious lives worthy of imitation.

Streamlined

A biblical alternative to becoming sidelined or flatlined is to become *streamlined*, as the writer of Hebrews suggests: "let us throw off everything that hinders and the sin that so easily entangles, and let us run with perseverance the race marked out for us" (Hebrews 12:1). Before a race in ancient Greece, runners would **shed tunics*** and robes that might slow them down or cause them to trip. Note that it is not only sin that is a problem; there are plenty of issues that, while not entangling us, can hinder us in a myriad of ways.

✳IN THE ORIGINAL OLYMPIC RACES, CONTESTANTS USUALLY RAN IN THE BUFF.

I am currently training for a **sprint triathlon***—a half-mile swim, twenty-two-mile bike ride and a three-and-a-half-mile run. This competition will be my first triathlon in several years, and I have managed to put on a few pounds in that span of time. Although I am somewhat fit in a cardiovascular sense, I have extra baggage that is slowing me down. So through my training and diet, I am reducing my on-board load and becoming more physically streamlined. Similarly, if we want to become spiritually streamlined, we must reduce our load of entanglements (sin) and hindrances that slow God's work in our life.

✳MY GOAL: TO NOT FINISH LAST.

The last thing I want to do is appoint myself a moral and ethical policeman. I understand the principle of Christian liberty. At the same time, I also know that more than a few youth workers have been sidelined or flatlined by exercising their Christian "liberty." The writer of Proverbs tells us:

> Above all else, guard your heart,
>   for it is the wellspring of life. (4:23)

The New Testament also contains numerous admonitions to guard our heart, mind and faith (check out Luke 6:43-45; 1 Corinthians 16:13; 1 Timothy 6:20; 2 Timothy 1:14). So let me suggest a few ways we can protect ourselves as we seek to become spiritually streamlined:

- We must guard our hearts from exposure to questionable input, especially movies, videos, magazines, TV and music. Youth workers sometimes expose themselves (often with sincere motives) to garbage and filth under the guise of better understanding contemporary youth culture. However, the benefits of cultural understanding are, unfortunately, often outweighed by decreased purity of heart.

- We must guard our lips from gossip, unwholesome talk, coarse jesting and the like. I hear far too many dirty jokes and unwholesome words coming out of the mouths of youth workers. I also hear more than a little "ministry talk" that more closely resembles gossip. The biblical admonition "Nor should there be obscenity, foolish talk or coarse joking" (Ephesians 5:4) must be taken literally.

- We must guard our physical bodies from breakdown. Abuse of my body has influenced my effectiveness in ministry more negatively than neglect of spiritual disciplines or lack of training. We need to quit taking the "bodily discipline is only of little profit" passage (1 Timothy 4:8 NASB) out of context in order to excuse laziness, obesity or bad habits. Healthy bodies enhance our ability to think and pray clearly, respond to stress, and survive those seasons of youth ministry when schedules go amuck.

- We must guard against broken relationships and unresolved conflict. If we are harboring anger or bitterness toward anyone, be it a student or parent, the senior pastor, a fellow youth worker, spouse, or child, we have given the devil a foothold (Ephesians 4:27) and have as much chance of attracting the blessing of God to our ministry as does the guy does who preaches with his mistress sitting in the congregation.

- We must guard our time with our family and the quality of our relationships with our spouse and children. There are more than a few elderly spiritual statesmen (notably Billy Graham) who have done amazing things for the kingdom yet have expressed a measure of regret at the corresponding neglect of their families.[5]

- We must guard our schedules, notably our devotional and prayer time. Bible study and message preparation time is not usually a good substitute for devotional time. We must also learn to "remember the Sabbath" (Exodus 20:8). This practice is not just a good idea; it's one of the Ten Commandments.

- We must guard ourselves with the full armor of God (Ephesians 6:10-18), not allowing fiery demonic darts to find their mark in cracks of disobedience. Nothing will sideline or flatline a youth worker faster than becoming a human dartboard in the tavern of hell.

Tom Phillips writes of the time someone once asked the British evangelist Gipsy Smith how to start a revival. "He replied, 'If you want to start a revival, go home and get a piece of chalk. Go inside your closet and draw a circle on the floor. Kneel down in the middle of the circle and ask God to start a revival inside the chalk mark. When He has answered your prayer, the revival has begun.' "[6]

Revival starts in our own lives. If we're not obediently pursuing holiness and allowing God to transform us, we can hardly expect our students to pursue holiness in their lives.

It's time to get out the chalk.

THREE

"I AM WOUNDED"

A Place for Healing

---

heal (hēl)

1. To restore to health or soundness; cure.
2. To set right; repair.
3. To restore to spiritual wholeness.

I was sitting on the banks of the Deschutes River in central Oregon on a warm July afternoon, waiting for the evening hatch to begin so I could once again "cast my fly upon the waters" in hopes of enticing large trout. Flyfishing for trout is a form of physical, emotional and spiritual therapy for me, a key component of my own ongoing youth-worker renewal regimen. But this time I was seeking more than renewal. I was badly hurt, with a self-inflicted wound of the soul that was draining the life out of me. I needed healing.

About a month earlier, I had resigned my youth pastorate after a pretty radical case of youth worker burnout. Fifteen years of "pedal to the metal" vocational youth ministry finally caught up with me, and most of what provided a measure of stability in my life—physically, mentally, emotionally and spiritually—picked up and went on vacation. The replacement guests were discouragement, depression, extreme fatigue and the haunting feeling that although I could have avoided this, I hadn't done so. On many occasions I had taught on the pitfalls of youth ministry, and now I was experiencing precisely what I had warned others about.

I had hit bottom several months earlier at a conference for youth workers that I had helped plan, where I was supposed to speak on the topic of longevity in youth ministry. Not real good timing on that one. I had imagined sharing some inspiring thoughts from my experiences as a local church "veteran," but when the time came for me to stand at the podium in front of my peers, my stomach was in knots, and so was my brain. I was more concerned about the distinct possibility of losing my sanity in front of my peers than inspiring them. Delivering my short and fuzzy message left me feeling even more drained.

Experiencing burnout was new territory for me. I had always considered myself emotionally stable. In fact, I had prided myself on my ability to "suck it up" and push a little harder when adversity arose. My attitude toward burnout was, "I doubt it'll happen to me because I'm pretty tough emotionally." Such an attitude only compounded the fear and shock I experienced when **I hit bottom.***

*SO MUCH FOR SUCKING IT UP.

After a few weeks on medical leave from my church, I crawled back in the ministry saddle again, only to be bucked off again five months later. I decided that to jump straight back into ministry again (if I even could) would be disingenuous, so with a wife fresh off two major surgeries, a three-year-old daughter and three-week-old son at home, and no immediate prospects for future employment, I resigned my youth pastorate. A few weeks later I ended up on the banks of the Deschutes after my two best buddies all but forced me to take the trip with them.

During that afternoon lull in the fishing, I picked up a book that one of the guys had brought along, randomly opened it and began reading. It didn't take long to get my attention: "The Bible everywhere teaches that God is underwhelmed by our best efforts and unimpressed with our most spectacular achievements. It's not what we do for Him that matters nor should it matter much to us. What matters most is what we are to Him."[1] The author, Dave Roper, referenced Luke 10:20, in which the disciples, home from a short missions trip, came to Jesus to report their successes. Jesus replies, "Do not rejoice that the spirits submit to you, but rejoice that your names are written in heaven." Roper comments, "The disciples felt good about themselves because they had done well. It was far better, Jesus observed, to get one's joy from the knowledge that we're special to God, that He knows our names and has them in His book!"[2]

I immediately grabbed my Bible, turned to Luke 10 and soaked in the passage. And at that moment in time I had an "aha" experience that changed me forever. I realized that my downfall had come as a result of my unconscious attempts to earn favor with God through my youth ministry prowess rather than simply enjoying the favor that he freely extended to me as his child. Correct works-versus-grace theology had always been fixed firmly in my head but until that day at the river had made only occasional visits to my heart. A truth that I had repeated to myself countless times—God is more concerned about who I am to him than what I do for him—finally began to settle deep within me, and the healing process began.

Wounded Healers

Henri Nouwen gave prominence to the phrase "wounded healer" when he wrote a well-known book with that title in the early seventies. The thesis of Nouwen's book is that in seeking to be messengers of healing and hope to a wounded, hopeless generation, we can do so only out of our own woundedness. Nouwen writes, "Thus like Jesus, he who proclaims liberation is called not only to care for his own wounds and the wounds of others, but also to make his wounds into a major source of his healing power."[3]

I resonate with Nouwen's statement, even though it doesn't fit with the traditional model of the put-together youth worker dispensing pearls of wisdom and words of comfort to those suffering from battlefield wounds. If we are going to persevere over the long haul in youth ministry, we are going to be wounded. The wounds may take the form of an emotional breakdown, or hurt from being undermined in our ministries by an unsympathetic senior pastor or angry parents, or the slow erosion of a marriage that struggles to withstand the time and energy assault that comes with youth ministry. Sometimes wounds are superficial and heal quickly, while other times they are incapacitating and require a lengthy healing process. But just as Jesus is able to sympathize with our weaknesses and dispense mercy and grace in our time of need because he was "tempted in every way, just as we are" (Hebrews 4:15), so we who are wounded are able to be sources of healing for our brothers and sisters in youth ministry.

When I hit bottom, God used his Word to begin my healing. But he also used his servants—my two buddies and my fellow youth workers—to minister powerfully to me with compassion and understanding. Not surprisingly, the people who ministered most effectively to me were wounded healers themselves. At the youth conference where I hit my lowest point, I met a guy who had burned out himself a few years earlier and had literally spent months in bed, curled up in a fetal position. I also met a woman who had been through the youth-ministry wringer with her husband, an experience that took a great toll on them physically and emotionally. This woman, understanding my pain, simply wrapped her arms around me and loved me. A few months later I ran into another of my wounded healers in the waiting room of a psychiatrist's office, an experience that was good for a few laughs.

As wounded healers, what we can, and must, dispense to our fellow youth workers is not primarily a prescription for ministry effectiveness but rather an antidote for success-based self-worth. Inside-out youth ministry is ultimately aimed at reaching emerging generations of youth, but it requires a growing army of youth workers who are secure in the fact that God is more concerned about who they are to him than what they do for him.

A Limping Army

I have always identified with Jacob. That is probably not a really good thing, since Jacob was one of the earliest purveyors of deceit and deception in the history of the world, but **I identify with him nevertheless.***

Jacob was one of the first wounded healers in the Bible. Before he was successfully reconciled with his brother Esau he had an all-night wrestling match with God that left him crippled in the hip and, ultimately, changed. I identify with him both in his struggles and in his woundedness. During the many dark nights of the soul that I experienced during my burnout, I too wrestled with God. And like Jacob, I came away both limping and changed—limping in that my supposed emotional invulnerability had been stripped away;

*ANY MORE SELF-DISCLOSURE ALONG THESE LINES WILL HAVE TO WAIT FOR ANOTHER BOOK.

changed in that I was now able to minister healing to others out of my own woundedness.

I suspect Jacob's limp was a continual reminder to him of both his former nature (as if his name wasn't enough—Jacob means "supplanter," which is what he tried to do right out of the womb when he grasped the heel of his first-born twin brother, Esau), and of the God who heals. My limp is of the emotional variety, not the physical. Most of the time I am not consciously aware of it, but on occasion the yellow caution flags that I missed the first several times (maybe one day I will *really* figure it out) appear, and **I remember.*** Although I have not had a major meltdown in many years (I had a few close calls in the first several years following my initial flameout), I know I am perfectly capable of another implosion.

*BOY, DO I REMEMBER.

The longer we remain in youth ministry, the greater the chance that we'll be wounded and, as a result, develop a limp. When that happens, we must embrace our limp and value it as a reminder that the God who heals will use us as wounded healers to minister to a wounded generation.

SELAH

*O sacred Head, now wounded, with grief and shame
   weighed down;*

*Now scornfully surrounded with thorns, Thy only
   crown;*

*How art Thou pale with anguish, with sore abuse and
   scorn;*

*How does that visage languish, which once was bright
   as morn!*

O Lord of life and glory, what bliss till now was Thine!

I read the wondrous story; I joy to call Thee mine.

*What Thou, my Lord, hast suffered was all for sinners'
   gain;*

*Mine, mine, was the transgression, but Thine the deadly
   pain.*

*What language shall I borrow to thank Thee, dearest
   Friend,*

For this Thy dying sorrow, Thy pity without end?

Oh, make me Thine forever; and, should I fainting be,

Lord, let me never, never outlive my love to Thee.

"O Sacred Heart, Now Wounded"
Bernard of Clairvaux (1091-1153)

A GIFT OF MERCY

---

mer•cy (mûr′sē)

1. Compassionate treatment, especially of those under one's power; clemency.
2. A disposition to be kind and forgiving.
3. Something for which to be thankful; a blessing.

I was perusing my junk mail when I came across a promotion for a journal on the Christian spiritual life. Curious, I split the tape and opened it up. My eyes immediately went to the following quote: "As we get older, perhaps we shed ideas and concepts until only a few simple words remain. *Mercy* remains."[1] *That's you, **dude!**** I exclaimed to myself.

When I was a college student and a new Christian, I learned the distinctions of God's justice, mercy and grace.

• Justice = getting what you deserve.

• Mercy = getting less than what you deserve.

• Grace = getting none of what you deserve.

These definitions may not be the stuff of theology books, but

*I REFER TO MYSELF AS **DUDE** TO REASSURE MYSELF **THAT I'M STILL CULTURALLY RELEVANT.**

they've stuck with me over the years, so they must be pretty good. Let's say, for example, that you're at basketball practice. You know that the penalty for goofing off is running ten laps. You goof off anyway.

- Justice = the coach making you run ten laps.
- Mercy = the coach making you run five laps.
- Grace = the coach running the ten laps for you.

We serve a God of justice, mercy and grace. His justice demands that our sinfulness be accounted for; the penalty is spiritual death. His mercy is evident in that we don't suffer immediately the eternal consequences of our sinfulness—God gives us time to repent and turn to him. By God's grace we don't have to pay the penalty for our sinfulness; Christ died on the cross on our behalf.

My prayers of late have involved a lot of thanking God for his mercy, but not exactly the mercy described above. I've experienced that type of mercy—for eighteen years I lived apart from God, and he mercifully withheld his judgment. But since I turned to God and repented of my sinfulness, I have still sinned in thoughts, attitudes and actions. I still face consequences, but I am very aware that God's mercy has often protected me from the full extent of those consequences.

We are works in progress. When we place our trust in Christ, we end one story and begin another, a lifelong process of becoming more like him. The Bible calls it being "conformed to the likeness of his Son" (Romans 8:29). Theologians call it *sanctification*. We will not be complete until we meet God face to face in glory. In the meantime we learn to practically implement faith, trust and obedience. The learning curve makes for mishaps along the way, but if we were to suffer the full consequences of our sins in the process of being conformed to Christ, we would all be legitimately in a world of hurt.

We also travel this road of sanctification in the midst of a fallen world, and as a result we sometimes suffer innocently the consequences of the world's sinfulness. People face disabilities, injuries, death and loss seemingly randomly. Their trials are particularly tragic because they bear some of the weight of sins committed long ago and far away—even as far back as the Garden of Eden. Justice demands that actions have consequences, and sinful actions on a cosmic scale can have cosmic consequences that spread throughout history and over all the earth. We can learn from people who remain thankful for God's mercy as they face the world's burden of God's justice.

Jack and I used to work together as youth pastors—he did junior high, I did high school—and he now serves on my board of directors at LINC Ministries. Jack broke his neck on a junior high water skiing trip and has been a quadriplegic ever since. Pain from the injury and subsequent surgeries keep him bedridden much of the time.

Phil and I roomed together in college, went to seminary together, and interned and pastored together at the same churches. Phil developed epilepsy around the time of Jack's accident. Medications and brain surgery have helped control his seizures but have not stopped them altogether. He hasn't driven a car in decades, and he could "blip out" (his phrase) at any time—even in the middle of a sermon.

Ron was another former roommate. He taught high school and worked as a wilderness guide during the summer. He loved kids passionately. Around the same time tragedy struck Jack and Phil, Ron died from cancer, leaving behind a grieving young bride.

Wally, a more recent acquaintance, is the former pastor of a large underground church in the Middle East. Wally was taken from his young family, tortured and sentenced to die for his faith before being miraculously released the day he was scheduled to be executed.

What is common to these four men, besides adversity, is a thankful heart. In the midst of their sufferings, they acknowledged God's mercy in their lives. When I am around them (and I need to be around them frequently), I remember to acknowledge God's mercy in my own life.

Youth ministers can get beaten down a lot. Parents don't like our methods, our senior pastor wonders why we don't attract more students, our spouse doesn't think we remember who they are, our kids cry when we leave the house for another evening activity, the bank calls to see when (or if) our mortgage check is coming, and kids we pour our lives into for years barely acknowledge our existence. Long hours of work, long lines of students to call, long lists of events to schedule and long-range planning to do leave us longing for relief. We're short on volunteers, short on cash, short on benefits and short on affirmation from people close to us, leaving us with short tempers and, too often, short stints in ministry.

But in reality, we have much for which to be thankful. The hymn "Great Is Thy Faithfulness" sums it up:

Morning by morning new mercies I see;
All I have needed Thy hand hath provided—
Great is Thy faithfulness, Lord, unto me!

Youth ministry is fraught with challenges, problems, frustrations and struggles. So is life. Only by God's inexhaustible mercy are we able to engage in life and ministry at the level we do. Mercy remains, indeed.

SECOND
MOVEMENT

RETHINKING
YOUR APPROACH

FOUR

"I AM SAFE"

A Stronghold of Protection

---

strong•hold (strông'hōld)

    1. A fortified place or a fortress.

    2. A place of survival or refuge.

David Wilcox's song "Eye of the Hurricane" tells the story of a woman who rides a fast motorcycle called the Hurricane to help her deal with life's problems (for her, a broken heart).[1] When she rides fast enough through a storm, there is an "eye" of protection behind the windshield that keeps her from getting wet. Similarly, speeding through the night on her motorcycle provides an "eye" of protection, or refuge, from her problems.

Storms in life are guaranteed, and when the gusts and gales come, most of us learn to weather them pretty well. Hurricanes, however, are a different story. We aren't built to withstand hurricanes. When they come—broken relationships, the loss of a job, a death in the family, serious illness, major disappointments, even demonic attack—we naturally seek an "eye" of safety. For some, the eye is found is substance abuse and addiction, TV and videos, sexual fantasies, overworking, or a host of other problems.

As people get older, they develop their own ways of finding, or constructing, eyes of safety from life's hurricanes. But students, who do not have much experience at finding "eyes" that

work, often turn to more potentially destructive options, usually because they don't know any better. That is one reason
why suicide and substance abuse are epidemic among young
people: they are quick escapes, or "eyes," from the hurricanes
of family dysfunction, abuse, **"puppy love,"*** peer group rejec-
tion and a host of other adolescent maladies. Of course, those
of us who are older find more "mature" ways of finding the
"eye"—alcohol, fantasies, emotional
affairs or perhaps overloading our
ministry schedule.

*MORE LIKE "PIT BULL LOVE" TO THEM.

Sometimes life's hurricanes result
from poor choices, but sometimes
they are just a part of life. A bestsell-
ing book a while back titled *Why Bad
Things Happen to Good People* seems
to imply that bad things should not happen to good people
and that there are people out there good enough to not have
bad things happen to them.

The reality, though, is that we are *all* sinful people who live
in a fallen world, and as such, we can, unfortunately, expect
bad stuff to show up more frequently than we would like. But
God is an "eye" available to us in the midst of any storm; he is
our stronghold. Although he does not always protect *from* the
storms of life (see Matthew 6:34; John 16:33; 2 Timothy 3:1), he
offers spiritual protection *in the midst of* the storms. An eye can
be a place of safety from the harmful effects of the hurricane,
but it is still part of the hurricane; actually, it's in the center of
the raging winds.

The apostle Paul experienced many hurricanes in his lifetime:

I have worked much harder, been in prison more frequently, been flogged more severely, and been exposed to death again and again. Five times I received from the Jews the forty lashes minus one. Three times I was beaten with rods, once I was stoned, three times I was shipwrecked, I spent a night and a day in the open sea, I have been constantly on the move. I have been in danger from rivers, in danger from bandits, in danger from my own countrymen, in danger from Gentiles; in danger in the city, in danger in the country, in danger at sea; and in danger from false brothers. I have labored and toiled and have often gone without sleep; I have known hunger and thirst and have often gone without food; I have been cold and naked. (2 Corinthians 11:23-27)

Yet Paul could also say that in the midst of the many storms of his life, he had found a stronghold or "eye" in the midst of all: "That is why, for Christ's sake, I delight in weaknesses, in insults, in hardships, in persecutions, in difficulties. For when I am weak, then I am strong" (2 Corinthians 12:10).

Life's hurricanes can build perseverance and character (see James 1), and they can refine our faith (1 Peter 1:6-7). Sometimes we don't know (and may never know this side of heaven) how they, and our place in the midst of them, are woven into the divine fabric of God's sovereign purposes. Nevertheless, they should prompt us to seek the spiritual "eye" that can be found in Christ alone. Other "eyes" can only supply temporary, and ultimately inadequate, protection.

Our task in youth ministry is to help students see that seeking refuge in counterfeit eyes is not necessary or, ultimately, effective. Christ, our true Refuge, who created us for the express purpose of an ongoing, intimate relationship with him, provides our eye in the midst of the storms of life. We who have experienced his peace, security, contentment and fulfillment living in the eye have the awesome responsibility of sharing this message with those who desperately need it.

A Stronghold for Youth Workers

Of course, not all of us are experienced at living in the eye. Youth ministry is a storm and hurricane magnet, and too often the storms and hurricanes get the best of us. If there's a youth worker out there who has not experienced significant storms, believe me, they are coming. You will experience many of the varieties of storms that others do, and in addition, you will experience some custom-made hurricanes. Francis Frangipane elaborates:

> The Bible tells us of a time when Satan shall be cast down to the earth. He will come, "having great wrath, knowing that he has only a short time" (Rev. 12:12). While some Christians question whether the church will be the victim of such hellish warfare, it is obvious even in our world today that the magnitude of evil has escalated.
>
> What is our response? Has God provided for us a Christian equivalent to the ark He provided Noah? Is there a spiritual Goshen where we can dwell in safety during God's judgments? We believe the answer to these questions is yes. God has provided spiritual protection for Christians, a stronghold where our souls can always find safe harbor.
>
> . . . Once we have found this place, nothing we encounter in life can defeat us; God Himself preserves us in all things. In every distress or devilish plot set against us, we

emerge the better for it. It is the redemptive power of Christ reversing the plans of Satan and annulling the effects of death in our lives.[2]

A stronghold is a literal or figurative fortress, such as the island city of Tyre. The city withstood a fifteen-year siege by Nebuchadnezzar and was never completely conquered until Alexander the Great did so over two centuries later, in 332 B.C. A stronghold is also a place of refuge. For example, the desert served as a stronghold for David as he sought protection from Saul (1 Samuel 23:14). But David knew well that a true stronghold was not found in a city or rocky outpost:

> The LORD is a refuge for the oppressed,
>   a stronghold in times of trouble. (Psalm 9:9)

> The LORD is my rock, my fortress and my deliverer;
>   my God is my rock, in whom I take refuge.
> He is my shield and the horn of my salvation, my
>   stronghold. (Psalm 18:2)

> The LORD is my light and my salvation—
>   whom shall I fear?
> The LORD is the stronghold of my life—
>   of whom shall I be afraid? (Psalm 27:1)

When the hurricanes of life assault us, there is a place, a spiritual stronghold, where we can find refuge in the midst of the storm—not necessarily protection from the hurricane, but strength, peace and perspective in the midst of it.

Over my years in ministry I have faced a variety of "hurricanes"—financial crises, health crises, emotional crises, ministry crises. Far too often I have sought refuge in a "second-best" stronghold. Part of my own inside-out renewal process (and it *is* a process, not an event) has been to learn to increasingly seek refuge in the stronghold of God. The yearning of my heart is to learn to *reside in*—not just visit—that stronghold.

In the stronghold of God you and I will find rest; we will find security and safety; we will be able to fight for the lives of the kids we love from a position of advantage and strength.

God is our refuge and strength,
    an ever-present help in trouble.
Therefore we will not fear, though the earth give way
    and the mountains fall into the heart of the sea,
though its waters roar and foam
    and the mountains quake with their surging.

Selah

There is a river whose streams make glad the city of God,
    the holy place where the Most High dwells.
God is within her, she will not fall;
    God will help her at break of day.
Nations are in uproar, kingdoms fall;
    he lifts his voice, the earth melts.

The LORD Almighty is with us;
    the God of Jacob is our fortress.

Selah

Come and see the works of the LORD,
    the desolations he has brought on the earth.
He makes wars cease to the ends of the earth;
    he breaks the bow and shatters the spear,
    he burns the shields with fire.
"Be still, and know that I am God;

I will be exalted among the nations,
I will be exalted in the earth."

The LORD Almighty is with us;
the God of Jacob is our fortress.

Selah
(Psalm 46)

"I AM AT REST"

A Blessing of Sabbath

---

rest (rĕst)

1. Cessation of work, exertion or activity.
2. Peace, ease or refreshment resulting from sleep or the cessation of activity.
3. Sleep or quiet relaxation.
4. Relief or freedom from disquiet or disturbance.
5. Mental or emotional tranquility.

Remember the Sabbath day by keeping it holy. Six days you shall labor and do all your work, but the seventh day is a Sabbath to the LORD your God. On it you shall not do any work, neither you, nor your son or daughter, nor your manservant or maidservant, nor your animals, nor the alien within your gates. For in six days the LORD made the heavens and the earth, the sea, and all that is in them, but he rested on the seventh day. Therefore the LORD blessed the Sabbath day and made it holy. (Exodus 20:8-11)

■　　　■　　　■

When I was young and single, youth ministry was pretty much a twenty-four/seven endeavor for me. Yeah, I was a bit of a workaholic, but honestly, I loved what I was doing so much that I didn't want it any differently. Hanging out on campus, coaching football at the local high school, discipling kids, meeting with my volunteer staff team, putting together weekly programs and messages, strategizing about reaching the schools in my community—I ate it all up. Other than occa-

sional forays to nearby rivers to cast flies at trout, I was a youth ministry machine. Marriage modi-
fied that lifestyle a bit; two children modified it still more. But it wasn't until **I went down*** in flames that I gave much thought to the foreign concepts of balance, rhythm and rest. I was too busy serving God to lie around the house for one whole day a week.

*IF YOU SKIPPED CHAPTER THREE, GO BACK AND READ IT FOR THE SORDID DETAILS.

Sabbath was a concept to which I had never given a whole lot of consideration. In my "work hard, play harder" lifestyle, a day of rest was an option not often exercised. But it's pretty hard to ignore the fourth commandment indefinitely.

"Why Do You Ask, Sweetheart?"
Time for honesty once again. I'd been dancing around the implications of the Sabbath for some time when my bride initiated a brief, pointed discussion: "Mike, have you read the commandment about the Sabbath lately?"

"Why do you ask, sweetheart?"

"Well, are we going to take our obedience seriously and consider some changes to our lifestyle, or should we just ignore that particular commandment?"

"Uh, well . . ." End of discussion.

Actually, it was the beginning of an ongoing discussion—one that continues to this day—about aligning our own lives and our family life with the commandment. The way I see it, there is the specific command as well as a big-picture principle to be considered. The specific command is rather, well, specific: one day of rest a week. The specific day is not necessarily the issue. For the Jews, the Sabbath was Saturday; since Christ's death and resurrection, Sunday has been the traditional Sabbath for Christians.

Where the issue of Sabbath gets dicey is trying to define *rest.* For my family, a day of rest means taking a break from the work that characterizes the other six days of our week. Since my other six days are characterized by vocational ministry stuff, I tried to stay completely away from anything ministry-related. But the adjustment has not come easy. In the beginning, I may have used a rest day to go on a bike ride with my family, but I also tended to sneak into my office to check my work-related e-mail or label and sort bulk mailings.

I am slowly learning a weekly rhythm of rest though. Now I've pretty much shut down my Sunday forays into the office. Terri lets the laundry sit, we bring in dinner so she doesn't have to cook, and we're working with our kids on how Sabbath affects their normal "terrorize the neighborhood" routine. Despite the adjustment these changes have required, I have come to love it this way. The funny thing is, I seem to be able to get as much ministry done in six days as I used to in seven, perhaps even more. E-mails are, amazingly, still in my computer when I check it Monday at 12:01 a.m. (Just kidding.) I feel little guilt falling asleep in my chair while watching a golf tournament.

Making It Real

Don't let me give the impression that these adjustments were easy for my family to make, or that they will be for you. For most youth workers, Sunday is the busiest day of the week, with a worship service, Sunday school, a youth staff meeting, discipleship with students, an evening service and so on. At one church where I served as youth pastor, the job description called for six days a week of work, which made taking a Sabbath even more of a challenge. Monday may be a day off and a possibility for a Sabbath, but with a spouse, kids, house, yard and cars all demanding our attention (and rightly so), how does one find rest?

That challenge will be magnified when trying to impart the principle and particulars of Sabbath to students who are under tremendous pressure from teachers, coaches, parents and sometimes youth workers to fit more and more into their hectic lives. For them to seriously consider Sabbath means making very difficult decisions. Some of them have already made difficult decisions to free up time to be involved in our ministries. If we as youth leaders (and parents) are not teaching *and* modeling Sabbath in a practical, workable fashion, how can we expect our students to give it a try?

I wish I could list for you a number of practical ways to integrate Sabbath into your life and ministry, but I'm still trying to make this real in my own life and ministry. I'm wary of falling into the same legalism that plagued the Pharisees, who were indignant at the disciples for picking heads of grain for a Sabbath snack. That being said, let me challenge you in just a few areas regarding the Sabbath:

- Undertake a word study of *Sabbath*. (If you are part of a church staff team, this would be a good project to do together. Be sure to include Isaiah 58:13-14.)
- Discuss the concept of Sabbath with your spouse. If you have a family, think about some creative ways you can integrate Sabbath into your schedule.
- Ask God to show you how *he* wants you to practice Sabbath.

Whatever you do, don't just ignore the issue of Sabbath (this will be your greatest temptation); after all, it *is* one of the Ten Commandments.

True Rest

Now it's time to address the big-picture Sabbath principle of rest that I mentioned earlier:

> There remains, then, a Sabbath-rest for the people of God; for anyone who enters God's rest also rests from his own work, just as God did from his. Let us, therefore, make every effort to enter that rest, so that no one will fall by following their example of disobedience. (Hebrews 4:9-11)

This passage is making two points. The first concerns salvation, which is not something we earn by our attempted acts of righteousness (being a good person, doing good works, even keeping the Sabbath). Rather, salvation comes through resting, by faith, in the person and work of Jesus Christ. Hebrews gives the example of the Israelites wandering in the wilderness, unable to enter the rest of Canaan for forty years because of their disobedience and failure to rest in God's promise of a "land flowing with milk and honey" (Exodus 3:8). Our own efforts don't get us into heaven, any more than the striving of the Israelites got them into the Promised Land; faith in the finished work of Christ is what gets us there.

✱SEE EPHESIANS 1—2 FOR A LENGTHY LIST OF SPIRITUAL BLESSINGS.

The second point concerns post-salvation and continuing to rest in God's finished work. Once we receive, by faith, the rest of salvation, we are the beneficiaries of many wonderful promises. We are the recipients of "every **spiritual blessing**✱ in Christ." In all things God works for the good of those who love him, and nothing can separate us from his love (see Romans 8:28-39). These promises, and many more like them, are not something we must strive to attain; they are ours for free! And because of that, we can rest from trying to earn God's favor or trying to rack up spiritual brownie points. And we no longer need to be held captive by fear, worry and anxiety, or guilt and self-condemnation. God's rest is something for us to enjoy *continually*.

Why, then, do I devote so much time and energy to "doing" stuff for God, stressing out about it far too much and not devoting nearly enough time to enjoying the blessings of being his child and being in his presence? I'm not talking about being lazy or irresponsible here; I am talking about working very hard for God, but *in an attitude of rest*. That comes a whole lot harder for me—and for most of us who grew up with the so-called Protestant work ethic—than taking a Sabbath day off each week. "Come to me, all you who are weary and burdened, and I will give you rest. Take my yolk upon you and learn from me, for I am gentle and humble in heart, and you will find rest for your souls. For my yoke is easy and my burden is light" (Matthew 11:28-30). As we rest, he will take care of the rest.

SIX

"I AM HERE"

A Posture for Hearing

---

hear (hîr)

1. To perceive (sound) by the ear.
2. To learn by hearing; be told by others.
3. To listen to attentively.
4. To listen to and consider favorably.

I had just finished a rather lengthy process of crafting vision and mission statements for one of the organizations I lead. To be honest, I liked the end products. They were clear, concise and to the point. But as I pondered the statements I had created, I received a not-too-gentle nudge from the Holy Spirit, who brought to mind a passage from the book of the Old Testament prophet **Zephaniah.*** In rebuking the rebellious nation of Judah, Zephaniah wrote that, among other problems, they would "neither seek the Lord nor inquire of Him" (1:6).

✳YOU PROBABLY READ ZEPHANIAH RECENTLY IN YOUR QUIET TIME. MAYBE NOT.

My nudge from God was not a rebuke for rebellion; rather, it was more in the form of a question: "Mike, do you really think you spent the necessary time asking me what your vision and mission statements should be, or is all this a product of your own training and experience-driven scheming?" My response mirrored the standard retort of my favorite cartoon dog, Astro[1]: "Roh-roh." God was once again reminding *me* (I am a slow learner) of the importance of a lifestyle that both *seeks the Lord* and *inquires of him*.

During the time of Zephaniah, Judah's failure to seek and inquire was not merely the result of good intentions gone astray, it was outright rebellion. That is not the case with most youth workers I know. But the Israelites who had entered Canaan for the first time several hundred years earlier were not in outright rebellion either when the people of Gibeon deceived them. Remember that story? The Israelites had just beaten the stuffing out of Jericho and Ai, and Gibeonites were freaked out that they would soon be the next victim. So they resorted to some trickery:

> They went as a delegation whose donkeys were loaded with worn-out sacks and old wineskins, cracked and mended. The men put worn and patched sandals on their feet and wore old clothes. All the bread of their food supply was dry and moldy. Then they went to Joshua in the camp at Gilgal and said to him and the men of Israel, "We have come from a distant country; make a treaty with us." (Joshua 9:4-6)

The passage goes on to say that "the men of Israel sampled their provisions [used human reasoning and judgment] but did not inquire of the LORD" (Joshua 9:14). And they ended up making a treaty with the Gibeonites, which was in direct disobedience to God's expressed purposes. Bad move. Their marching orders were to utterly destroy the inhabitants of the land. Why? Because God knew that if they cohabited with the resident peoples, they would eventually co-mingle with them, adopt their wicked practices and rebel against him. And we all know that's exactly what happened. The overt examples of this didn't appear for a few generations, but this was the first crack in a foundation of obedience that would eventually crumble. The books of Judges, 1-2 Samuel, 1-2 Kings and 1-2 Chronicles give ample evidence that during the next several hundred years, when the nation of Israel inquired of the Lord, they were the recipients of a revelation of divine strategy and were victorious over their enemies; when they failed to do so, he left them to their own devices, and they usually got thrashed.

Does this have application to contemporary youth ministry? I have noticed that we youth workers tend to make great plans for God and ask him to bless those plans, rather than asking him for the plans in the first place. (I speak from my own experience here.) Could it be that youth ministry has not had a greater impact on youth and their culture in part because we have not persistently, consistently inquired of the Lord as to what to do to reach them? And could we results-oriented youth workers be guilty as well of seeking *stuff* from God (answers, blessings, famous ministries, budgets over $100, etc.) instead of seeking him alone?

God has a custom-tailored ministry strategy for each and every youth group or ministry network or city movement in our nation and our world. And that strategy is not primarily discovered by going to the Christian bookstore and picking up **the latest youth ministry book*** or by attending another conference or by getting more training. Those means are important, and I utilize them myself. But what worked for the Israelites in conquering Jericho was different than what worked in conquering Ai (see Joshua 6—8) or the other cities they came against. Similarly, what works in my youth ministry may not work in yours.

✱EXCEPT THIS BOOK, OF COURSE!

What works in Portland, Oregon, does not necessarily work in Portland, Maine. There are transferable principles of ministry, to be sure. But I am convinced that seeking the Lord and inquiring of him are the keys to his releasing the divine strategy that will influence the youth of our specific ministries and of the cities for which so many of us pray.

Seeking Versus Inquiring

As a father, I want my kids to love me for who I am to them more than for what I do for them. The same is true for our heavenly Father. Now let's be real: our kids are usually more interested in what we can do for them, right? But as they grow older, we pray that they will place more emphasis on who we are to them.

God understands our requests for him to do stuff for us. He wants to answer our prayers. He wants to use you and me to reach a generation of young people. He wants us to engage in the modern-day equivalent of withering fig trees and throwing mountains into the sea (Matthew 21:18-22). But his foremost desire is that we come to him primarily for who he is *to* us rather than for what he does *for* us. "Seeking his face" (a common biblical injunction) should take priority over "seeking his hand" of blessing.

For David and other biblical witnesses, seeking that relationship with God was of paramount importance. Inquiring of him was important—the danger of seeking yet not inquiring was, and is, very real—but the relationship was of primary importance.

> One thing I ask of the LORD,
>   this is what I seek:
> that I may dwell in the house of the LORD

all the days of my life,
to gaze upon the beauty of the LORD
and to seek him in his temple. (Psalm 27:4)

O God, you are my God,
   earnestly I seek you;
my soul thirsts for you,
   my body longs for you,
in a dry and weary land
   where there is no water. (Psalm 63:1)

When we seek God and worship him alone, he releases his blessing on us (see Psalm 24; 133), and as we experience God's blessing and begin to inquire of him, he reveals to us his divine strategy for our ministry.

According to the biblical pattern, divine strategy is progressively revealed. God doesn't give us the full meal deal at once; he feeds it to us one course at a time. His purposes are never static; new wine requires new wineskins. And so God is vitally interested in us *continually* seeking him and *continually* inquiring of him. He wants us, corporately and individually, to be *continually* dependent on him alone. When we are, he will use us in amazing ways.

The lions may grow weak and hungry,
   but those who seek the LORD lack no good thing.
(Psalm 34:10)

You will seek me and find me when you seek me with all your heart. (Jeremiah 29:13)

Learning to Hear God's Voice
When I was a new believer in college, I was taught various

ways to "hear" God through prayer, the Word, the counsel of other believers, circumstances and so on. To my recollection I was not taught that God could (and actually wanted to) speak to me in a voice that I could discern. I have since learned otherwise.

As we seek the Lord and inquire of him, *God wants us to learn to hear his voice.* He wants us to be modern-day Samuels who learn to hear that "gentle whisper" after a little practice:

The boy Samuel ministered before the LORD under Eli. In those days the word of the LORD was rare; there were not many visions.

One night Eli, whose eyes were becoming so weak that he could barely see, was lying down in his usual place. The lamp of God had not yet gone out, and Samuel was lying down in the temple of the LORD, where the ark of God was. Then the LORD called Samuel.

Samuel answered, "Here I am." And he ran to Eli and said, "Here I am; you called me."

But Eli said, "I did not call; go back and lie down." So he went and lay down.

Again the LORD called, "Samuel!" And Samuel got up and went to Eli and said, "Here I am; you called me."

"My son," Eli said, "I did not call; go back and lie down."

Now Samuel did not yet know the LORD: The word of the LORD had not yet been revealed to him.

The LORD called Samuel a third time, and Samuel got up and went to Eli and said, "Here I am; you called me."

Then Eli realized that the LORD was calling the boy. So Eli told Samuel, "Go and lie down, and if he calls you, say, 'Speak, LORD, for your servant is listening.' " So Samuel went and lay down in his place.

The LORD came and stood there, calling as at the other times, "Samuel! Samuel!"

Then Samuel said, "Speak, for your servant is listening." (1 Samuel 3:1-10)

When I slow down enough, quieting the noise that usually fills my head, and put myself in a listening posture, I can actually discern God's voice. Francis Frangipane comments:

> We too must learn to hear the voice of Him who rarely speaks audibly and observe the actions of Him who is otherwise invisible. . . . He will not fight for our attention; He must be sought. He will not startle us; He must be perceived. It took no special skill to "discern" the earthquake, the fire, or the great storm. But to sense the holy quiet of God, our other activities must cease.[2]

Frangipane is alluding to a passage found in 1 Kings 18—19, in which the prophet Elijah, fresh off the successful "dueling altars" episode with the prophets of Baal, is intimidated by an enraged Jezebel and runs for his life. He eventually ends up in a cave at Horeb, the mountain of God, where he discovers that the voice of God is not found in a great wind or an earthquake or fire, but in a "gentle whisper" (1 Kings 19:12). We, too, can hear that gentle whisper if we take the time to listen. And when we do, we will hear wonderful things. Sometimes the whisper will concern ministry vision or strategy; at other times, the whisper of the Spirit will be a word of personal encouragement or gentle correction, or perhaps just "I love you." What joyful renewal when the ears of our spirits learn to hear the voice of God!

SEVEN

"I AM A WARRIOR"

A Briefing on the Battle (I)

---

war•fare (wôr'fâr')

1. The waging of war against an enemy; armed conflict.
2. Military operations marked by a specific characteristic.
3. A state of disharmony or conflict; strife.
4. Acts undertaken to destroy or undermine the strength of another.

I hope you can deal with that huge bull's-eye you now have on your back, Higgs."

My friend and I were walking from the convention center to our hotel after another intense day in the prayer room of a youth evangelism conference. We were in the initial throes of a prayer team "unity meltdown," and as the leader, I was in major damage control mode. In addition, several of us on the prayer team had sensed the Spirit moving us to suggest to the conference leadership some rather radical adjustments to what was planned for the remainder of the event. I had not slept a wink the previous night, and my friend could tell that I was one whipped puppy, so his comment was not exactly a balm of healing at the time. In hindsight, though, it was both accurate and insightful. I am engaged in a spiritual battle. Though I don't particularly like it, and I often fight against it, I am learning to deal with it—something all of us in youth ministry need to do.

Twenty years ago, if you mentioned Satan to Joe Youth Worker, it would probably have conjured up images of a little guy in a red suit with horns, a pitchfork and a silly grin. Fortunately, that's not the case any more. Most people in student ministry now understand the reality of spiritual warfare and Satan's schemes.

Sometimes it's hard to remember that just a few decades ago, there was very little written on the subject of spiritual warfare except for a few somewhat obscure texts. Now there are scores of books on the subject, including several that target youth and those who work with them. And after the typical swinging from one extreme to the other, the church has adopted what seems to be a balanced and biblical perspective on spiritual warfare. Fulfilling the Great Commission, the church has come to understand, involves big-time warfare, a spiritual battle for the lives of billions involving spiritual strongholds, principalities and powers, and an aggressive engagement with spiritual weapons.

A balanced, biblical understanding of spiritual warfare is crucial to effective youth ministry. It's also critical since revival is more of a possibility now than at any other time in our lives so far. We live in days of unprecedented opportunity to advance the kingdom of God, with an unusual working or outpouring of the Holy Spirit in many places and in many ways. However, biblical principle and practical reality teach us that unprecedented opportunity and unusual outpouring result in unrelenting opposition from the enemy of our souls. Not that enemy opposition to the advancement of the kingdom of God ever relents; he is always at work, seeking to blind the minds of unbelievers (2 Corinthians 4:4), outwit believers (2 Corinthians 2:11), prowling around like a roaring lion looking for someone to devour (1 Peter 5:8) and even masquerading as an angel of light (2 Corinthians 11:14). But when the kingdom is on the move, the enemy will not go away quietly or lie down before us.

Youth ministry is among the most strategic ministries in the church, in part because the vast majority of decisions for Christ are made before the age of twenty. Guess who else knows that? You don't have to be very discerning to pick up that youth workers are particularly vulnerable to satanic activity. The more youth workers that can be taken out of the picture or rendered ineffective by the enemy, through whatever means possible, the more damage he can do against the kingdom. His ultimate desire and goal is to destroy us. Along the way, he will also seek to distract, discourage, derail, depress or disillusion us. Two personal examples will help illustrate that point.

Over the period of several months in the early 1980s, the adult leaders of my youth ministry started dropping like flies. Offering a variety of explanations, several volunteers left the team in the space of a few weeks, and some others seemed to be just going through the motions. **I attributed it all *** to a lack of commitment, my failure to consistently motivate, or normal youth staff attrition.

A few weeks later, I received a call from a former pastoral colleague who had left our church to begin a ministry that had to do with "spiritual warfare"—a well-known concept now but pretty new back then. He said we needed to discuss the reasons behind the loss of my volunteers. His counseling had uncovered the source of their problems: spiritual oppression, which in turn was traced to a woman who had been very active in our youth ministry the previous year. This young women, who came from a Christian family, had

*I'M A HIGHLY DISCERNING AND SENSITIVE KIND OF GUY.

started dabbling in the occult while in college, and ended up jumping into Satanism with both feet. Upon her return home, she started messing spiritually with several staff members who knew her well, including my wife and me. Several pretty wild counseling sessions with her confirmed this. Once the nature of the attacks were identified and broken, all the youth leaders returned to our team—with a quantum leap in their understanding of spiritual warfare. But if the schemes of the enemy had not been uncovered, who knows what would have happened.

Several years and one church later, I found myself horizontal in a reclining chair in our living room, enjoying a morphine buzz that followed surgery to repair a torn Achilles tendon. My stupor was interrupted when Pat, my junior high intern, appeared at our door. He had a young man from our college group in tow, and an obviously freaked-out female junior higher. The girl, from a family with some occultic connections, had dabbled in it a little herself, and now she wanted out.

Morphine had rendered me only partially rational, so Pat and my bride headed to the back room for some serious warfare and the beginning of a journey that lasted nearly a year. The *Reader's Digest* version includes a belligerent mom and a dad in denial; a car chase to the airport; jail time for the college student, who turned out to be more than just a friend to the young girl; and fellow pastoral staff members who were skeptical about spiritual warfare and wondering what kind of mess I had stirred up at our church. It was a frustrating, draining situation that wouldn't go away for a long, long time.

I'm not saying that it is normal for youth workers to be harassed by folks who are in the occult or to engage in car chases to the airport to stop junior high girls from being illegally taken across state lines. These, admittedly, are extreme examples; the explosive argument between you and your spouse that comes out of nowhere when you're trying to get your family loaded in the car for church, or the temptation to visit that porn site on the Web just once to see if it's really that bad, can be just as demonic (and destructive) as witches and curses. No matter what the overt symptoms of attack may be, a laissez-faire approach by ministries to spiritual warfare is an open invitation to minimal fruitfulness or a major-league thrashing, both courtesy of the adversary.

Let's be straight: if you are a youth worker engaged in significant kingdom work, you have a bull's-eye on you as well. So it is best to understand the nature of the battle, realize the covering of protection we have in Christ and be equipped to engage the enemy with success. Yet we must do so with a sense of biblical balance. As I stated earlier, Christendom tends to swing from one extreme to the other when it comes to this kind of stuff. John Dawson offers a healthy perspective here:

> Our prime objective, therefore, in intercession and spiritual warfare, is not the removal of the enemy, but the return of the glory. The restoration of God's needed favor. When we encounter a spiritual stronghold, it is not a testimony to the presence of a *big* demon, but rather to the absence of the glory of God. Just as nature abhors a vacuum, so it is in the unseen realm. When the glory departs, the demons rush in.
>
> My biggest problem is not demons. I am my biggest problem. It is only when God has cleansed my own wicked heart that participation in the redeeming work of intercession becomes possible. It is then that the power to change history is released through prayer.[1]

The Nature of the Battle: From Ignorance to Awareness

Scripture reminds us that our battle for the souls of young people is not merely "against flesh and blood, but against the rulers, against the authorities, against the powers of this dark world and against the spiritual forces of evil in the heavenly realms" (Ephesians 6:12). And as we engage in this battle, we are to be aware of demonic schemes "in order that Satan might not outwit us" (2 Corinthians 2:11).

So what are Satan's schemes? On a corporate level, they include destroying the church, or rendering it ineffective at making disciples and fulfilling the Great Commission. The evidence: local church struggles, factions and splits; denominational battles; competition among organizations or within communities.

On a personal level, the schemes are similar: destroy you and your relationship with God or render you ineffective for kingdom service or keep you in spiritual darkness and bondage. The enemy will seek to accomplish this in a variety of ways, including

- getting you to ignore the degree and subtlety of his influence (2 Corinthians 2:11)
- tempting you (Matthew 4:1-11; 1 Corinthians 7:5; 1 Thessalonians 3:5)
- accusing you falsely (Revelation 12:10)
- physically afflicting you (Job; 2 Corinthians 12:7-10)
- deceiving you by subtly twisting God's truth (2 Corinthians 11:13-15; 1 John 4:1-3; 2 John 7-11)
- dividing relationships (2 Corinthians 2:10-11; Ephesians 4:25-27)
- opposing you in ministry (Acts 13:6-12)

The Covering of Christ

Increased awareness of the nature of our spiritual battle can cause fear to creep into our hearts. This, too, is a strategy of the enemy, who would like nothing more than to see us immobilized or incapacitated by fear. In the story I mentioned previously about the attack on volunteers in my ministry, I was subsequently steered by my friend to read one of the few books about spiritual warfare that was in print at that time. At that point I had what can best be described as my first "power encounter" with the enemy. As I sat in my office reading the book, a sudden, overwhelming fear gripped me as the hair on my arms stood on end, and I found it increasingly difficult to breathe.

Discernment is not one of my stronger spiritual gifts, but I knew that I was not alone in that room. So did I slap on the full armor of God and engage in battle? **Nope.*** I bolted from my chair, running out the door and down the sidewalk, gasping for breath. I did eventually get my act together, and in the power encounters I have experienced in the ensuing years (some overt, some very subtle) I have been able to engage with a measure of effectiveness.

An early key in my ongoing transformation from pansy private to fledgling warrior in God's army has been my understanding of the spiritual protection and covering I have in Christ. Bible teacher

*I FREAKED.

Lance Lambert writes, "In these days when the Lord is calling the church around the world to battle stations, we need more than ever to understand our enemy. We also need to understand the rules of battle and how to fight from a place of complete safety and protection."[2]

While spiritual protection is a theme that runs throughout

the Bible, it is the focus of Psalm 91, enough so that I'm including the entire text below:

> He who dwells in the shelter of the Most High
> > will rest in the shadow of the Almighty.
> I will say of the LORD, "He is my refuge and my fortress,
> > my God, in whom I trust."

> Surely he will save you from the fowler's snare
> > and from the deadly pestilence.
> He will cover you with his feathers,
> > and under his wings you will find refuge;
> > his faithfulness will be your shield and rampart.
> You will not fear the terror of night,
> > nor the arrow that flies by day,
> nor the pestilence that stalks in the darkness,
> > nor the plague that destroys at midday.
> A thousand may fall at your side,
> > ten thousand at your right hand,
> > but it will not come near you.
> You will only observe with your eyes
> > and see the punishment of the wicked.

> If you make the Most High your dwelling—
> > even the LORD, who is my refuge—
> then no harm will befall you,
> > no disaster will come near your tent.
> For he will command his angels concerning you
> > to guard you in all your ways;
> they will lift you up in their hands,
> > so that you will not strike your foot against a stone.
> You will tread upon the lion and the cobra;
> > you will trample the great lion and the serpent.

"Because he loves me," says the LORD, "I will rescue him;
  I will protect him, for he acknowledges my name.
He will call upon me, and I will answer him;
  I will be with him in trouble,
  I will deliver him and honor him.
With long life will I satisfy him
  and show him my salvation."

The spiritual covering described here in such vivid detail is found as we "dwell in the shelter" of God, where fear is banished, protection is secured, angelic assistance is afforded, and spiritual authority is imparted. This is the place the enemy wants to keep us from. Lambert comments:

> Satan's great objective and strategy, both for the child of God and for the church of God, is to get us "uncovered," that is, out of our place of safety in the Lord. Satan knows that he cannot do anything against an individual or church when they are "abiding under the shadow of the Almighty," or, to use New Testament terms, abiding or remaining in Christ (John 15:1-8). Whilst we abide in Christ, Satan cannot reach us. He has to meet with Christ first. He meets the authority, the righteousness, the power, the mercy, the grace, the work of Christ. He meets it all before he can get at the believer. When we abide in Christ we have wonderful safety.[3]

As youth workers, one of the first things we teach students is the importance and practice of abiding in Christ. It's a truth we need to remind ourselves as well. I have found that habitually practicing the following four steps helps me to remain in a position of spiritual covering and protects the bull's-eye on my back:

1. *Confess quickly.* Don't give the enemy a foothold (Ephesians 4:26-27; 1 John 1:9).

2. *Forget totally.* The accuser will remind us of our sins. God "forgets" them (Psalm 103:11-12; Romans 4:7); so should we.

3. *Live obediently.* Putting on "the full armor of God" (Ephesians 6) boils down to a practical application of biblical truth—living out what we believe to be true.

4. *Pray aggressively.* Our lives are appropriate subjects for prayer (Ephesians 6:18). Peter Wagner comments, "The central, foundational activity for spiritual warfare is prayer. In one sense prayer is a weapon of warfare, and in another sense it is the medium through which all the other weapons are utilized."[4]

EIGHT
"I AM NOT ALONE"
A Briefing on the Battle (II)

re•in•force•ment (rē'ĭn-fôrs'mənt)

1. The act or process of reinforcing or the state of being rein-
   forced.
2. Something that reinforces.
3. Often *reinforcements.* Additional personnel or equipment sent
   to support a military action.

It's time for you to come to New Hampshire."

Cool. I had never been to New England in the fall when the
leaves were turning. It would be a great time for a family vacation: check out the fall colors, head down to see Boston and
Plymouth Rock, maybe drive up to Maine and crash the Bush
compound in Kennebunkport. But this was not a vacation.
This was me clearing my schedule, packing up my wife and
two kids, booking four round-trip tickets on a few weeks' no-
tice, and literally flying across the country to spend three very
intense days with two of our intercessors. The color of fall
leaves aside, I never would have gone unless I knew the invitation was not just from them but also from God. And I never
would have gone if I was not absolutely convinced of our need
for the additional spiritual covering and protection that intercessors can provide.

Paul understood better than most people what it means to
abide in the stronghold of Christ, yet his writings are peppered
with requests for prayer for protection:

I urge you, brothers, by our Lord Jesus Christ and by the love of the Spirit, to join me in my struggle by praying to God for me. Pray that I may be rescued from the unbelievers in Judea and that my service in Jerusalem may be acceptable to the saints there. (Romans 15:30-31)

For I know that through your prayers and the help given by the Spirit of Jesus Christ, what has happened to me will turn out for my deliverance. (Philippians 1:19)

And pray that we may be delivered from wicked and evil men, for not everyone has faith. (2 Thessalonians 3:2)

My personal favorite is 2 Corinthians 1:8-11:

We do not want you to be uninformed, brothers, about the hardships we suffered in the province of Asia. We were under great pressure, far beyond our ability to endure, so that we despaired even of life. Indeed, in our hearts we felt the sentence of death. But this happened that we might not rely on ourselves but on God, who raises the dead. He has delivered us from such a deadly peril, and he will deliver us. On him we have set our hope that he will continue to deliver us, as you help us by your prayers. Then many will give thanks on our behalf for the gracious favor granted us in answer to the prayers of many. (2 Corinthians 1:8-11)

Although Paul knew his protection ultimately came from Christ, he also knew that God uses the prayers of his people to supplement that protection. This is clear in the familiar Ephesians 6 passage concerning spiritual armor. Paul takes great pains to describe the various elements of our armor—the belt of truth, the breastplate of righteousness, the feet fitted with readiness from the gospel, the shield of faith, the helmet of salvation, the sword of the Spirit—all of which are afforded us as we abide in the stronghold of Christ. (In fact, the armor is Christ himself; see Romans 13:14.) Yet he follows this with a description of the role of prayer in spiritual protection that is both instructive and personal:

> And pray in the Spirit on all occasions with all kinds of prayers and requests. With this in mind, be alert and always keep on praying for all the saints.
>
> Pray also for me, that whenever I open my mouth, words may be given me so that I will fearlessly make known the mystery of the gospel, for which I am an ambassador in chains. Pray that I may declare it fearlessly, as I should. (Ephesians 6:18-20)

Paul considers personal prayer to be an essential offensive spiritual weapon at our disposal, but he considers the intercession of others on our behalf to be critically important as well.

While Scripture is not clear concerning the extent to which Paul had an organized team of prayer supporters, it is clear that the supplemental covering provided by the intercession of others is a necessity for those of us with bull's-eyes on our backs. Peter Wagner writes, "The most underutilized source of spiritual power in our churches today is intercession for Christian leaders."[1] Bo Boshears concurs:

> I'll never forget a gift I received from a student leader in southern California. This mature, godly young woman gave me a gift of prayer: the commitment to pray for my family, the ministry, and me every day for an entire year. She followed up by regularly adding new prayer requests to her list. Her gift marked my life and my ministry.

That experience showed me the value and power of prayer in a new way. I decided from then on that I would search for a few men and women each ministry season who would commit to pray for me and the ministry. Building a prayer team has become a meaningful, vital part of my ministry. The prayers of these men and women have no doubt covered and protected me over the years. Without this prayer cover, I know I would be more susceptible to the attacks of the Enemy. Their desire to support the ministry through prayer is invaluable to me.[2]

As I have taught about the development of a prayer team (Peter Wagner calls it a Prayer Shield) to many groups of youth workers, three common questions have surfaced.

1. How many prayer supporters do I need? My prayer team numbers **close to one hundred.*** Peter Wagner has hundreds and Bill Bright estimates his to be in the thousands. The principle of inquiring is helpful here: ask the Lord how many are to comprise your prayer team, and more important, who they are. I have a good friend who did this and was instructed by the Lord to seek "sixty swordsmen" (Song of Solomon 3:7-8) to pray regularly for him!

*THE MORE THE MERRIER!

2. Are there different levels of prayer support? Wagner's support consists of three levels of personal intercessors, with varying prayer assignments.[3] I have two levels on my team, but the point is not the number of levels but, rather, the reason for different levels. What I call Level One consists of the folks who have committed to pray for my family, my ministry and me on some sort of consistent basis. They don't necessarily go into their prayer closets each day and travail in prayer for me, and they may not know all the details of the needs of my family, my ministry or myself. But they pray, and I need them desperately.

What I call Level Two consists of a much smaller number of people, around a dozen, who feel a special call from the Lord to intercede for me more than casually. In many cases these folks are gifted as intercessors. Because of their commitment and giftedness, they need more fodder to fuel their praying, so I give them more information about prayer needs and issues. I also make sure our communication is two-way, which leads to the third question.

3. How do I communicate with my prayer supporters? The Internet has made communication almost instantaneous, and I frequently communicate with people in both levels of my team, corporately and individually, via e-mail. But there are more than a few senior citizens on my team who have not yet entered cyberspace, and these men and women of God are among the best prayer warriors I have! So I do a quarterly snail mailing to my entire team, and then supplement it with more frequent e-mails. And no matter what my means of communication, I try to keep it **simple.** * If I can identify five or six key areas in my ministry and my family life for which most of my team is interceding, I'm in pretty good shape. If folks want more, they usually ask for it, and I am happy to oblige.

One additional comment about communication: I make

> *CALL ME BACKSLIDDEN, BUT WHEN I RECEIVE A FEW DOZEN PRAYER REQUESTS, I USUALLY DON'T COVER THEM ALL.

sure that my Level Two folks know that I want (and need) to hear from them! I not only desire their fervent intercession, I also want to hear what the Lord is saying to them about my family, my ministry and me. I packed my family up and headed for New Hampshire not because God directly told me to do so, but because he told two of my intercessors that I should do so. I trusted them, and God confirmed their discernment in my own spirit, so we made the trip. That trip was unbelievably powerful and productive, and a very significant spiritual milestone for my family and me. Time and time again God has spoken in significant and strategic ways through my intercessors.

Covering Your Family and Home

When I am away from home on a ministry assignment, my family sometimes gets a measure of spiritual harassment. Sometimes my wife is awakened in the night with the sense that she is not alone; my son has struggled with nightmares, and my daughter has dealt with a variety of fears. To be sure, some of this is just "life," but without question much of it is connected to what I do. And the attacks are not just confined to times when I am absent. I have spent many nighttime hours praying through our home, interceding for my family and engaging in direct warfare.

While the experience of our family is not necessarily typical, the enemy *will* come at your home and family. And since he is a master of deceit and deception, the attacks will often be subtle or in the form of something that could be explained away, for example, sicknesses, nightmares, arguments, temptations. As I have struggled with our attacks, I have learned two key principles that have brought a significant measure of victory in this area. First, I have been continually reminded that I have significant *spiritual authority* that I can exercise to provide protection and covering for my family. I have understood this biblically for some time but have been slow in exercising it through my praying.

Second, I have learned that if I will ask, the Lord will show me (or my wife or my intercessors or even, on occasion, my children) if a particular problem at home has its source in the wiles of the enemy or in a case of bad take-out Chinese food. Alice and Eddie Smith of the U.S. Prayer Center have compiled a list of possible symptoms of a "spiritually polluted atmosphere" that require spiritual cleansing:

- sudden chronic illness
- recurrent bad dreams and nightmares
- insomnia or unusual sleepiness
- behavioral problems
- relational problems—continual fighting, arguing and misinterpreted communication
- lack of peace
- restless, disturbed children
- unexplained illnesses or bondage to sin
- ghosts or demonic apparitions (to which young children are particularly susceptible)
- poltergeists (the movement of physical objects by demons)
- foul, unexplainable odors
- atmospheric heaviness, making it hard to breathe
- continual nausea and headaches[4]

Prayer leader Chuck Pierce comments on this list, "If you are experiencing any of these things on an ongoing basis, ask the Lord to reveal any spiritual darkness that may be in your home. Remember that Jesus has given us authority over these beings and that He is far greater than any force that might come against you. There is no need to fear."[5] The danger of giving the devil too much credit is, in my mind, dwarfed by the danger of not recognizing his schemes. A spiritually protected home and family can be a wonderful place of refuge and rest, but we must realize that the enemy knows that too and will do all he can to disrupt it.

Living with a Bull's-eye

Like it or not, youth ministry is spiritual warfare, and we who comprise God's army in this cosmic clash must learn to deal with the bull's-eyes on our backs. So let's be aware of the bull's-eyes, properly equip ourselves to do battle against the spiritual forces of darkness that take aim at us, and contend in battle for the lives of the emerging generations of young people. Rise up, O men and women of God!

SELAH

God is my strong salvation; what foe have I to fear?
In darkness and temptation my light, my help is near.

*Though hosts encamp around me firm to the fight I
   stand;*
*What terror can confound me, with God at my right
   hand?*

Place on the Lord reliance, my soul, with courage wait;
His truth be thine affiance, when faint and desolate.

*His might thy heart shall strengthen, His love thy joy in-
   crease;*
*Mercy thy days shall lengthen; the Lord will give thee
   peace.*

"GOD IS MY STRONG SALVATION"
JAMES MONTGOMERY (1771-1854)

A CHALLENGE TO PERSEVERANCE

---

per•se•vere (pûr′sə-vîr′)

To persist in or remain constant to a purpose, an idea or a task in the face of obstacles or discouragement.

I served for a number of years as prayer director for the DC/LA Youth Evangelism Superconferences, where I had the opportunity to observe a growing trend: students at these conferences, as well as other similar conferences, are playing an increasingly prominent role—not just as participants but also as speakers, musicians and dramatists. And the students do not disappoint; there is little, if any, drop in the quality of the music or message.

These students—teens at the start of the new millennium—are part of what many are calling the "Joshua Generation" for their willingness to take spiritual leadership seriously when it comes to reaching their peers. Students in this generation are acting with initiative to organize conferences and evangelistic rallies, start campus clubs, mobilize prayer teams and live out their faith in radical yet real ways.

The moniker "Joshua Generation," of course, ties this generation to the man who led the Israelites out of the desert where they had spent the past forty years wandering, and into possession of the inheritance God had promised to their ancestor Abraham hundreds of years earlier. The courageous, aggressive leadership of Joshua is a wonderful model for today's passionate youth, who see their school campuses and their peers as their "promised inheritance."

Joshua was one of the original twelve spies sent out by Moses to explore the Promised Land. And unlike almost all of his companions, who were intimidated by the NBA player-sized inhabitants ("We seemed like grasshoppers in our own eyes, and we looked the same to them" [Numbers 13:33]) and urged a return to Egypt, Joshua strongly argued that the Israelites' God was much bigger than a bunch of eight-footers and that Israel's possession was ready for the taking.

But he wasn't the only one to argue that way.

Caleb

Caleb doesn't get a whole lot of ink in the Bible (thirty-four verses, to be exact), while Joshua racks up a few hundred, not to mention a book named for him. Yet it was Caleb who spoke up first about the Promised Land: "Then Caleb silenced the people before Moses and said, 'We should go up and take possession of the land, for we can certainly do it' " (Numbers 13:30). And Caleb was the one initially commended by God for his courageous faith: "But because my servant Caleb has a different spirit and follows me wholeheartedly, I will bring him into the land he went to, and his descendants will inherit it" (Numbers 14:24).

We don't hear a whole lot more about Caleb after that; he is out of the spotlight until well after Joshua leads his countrymen to their initial conquest of the land. But he pops up again in Joshua 14, asking Joshua for the inheritance he was promised so many years ago:

So here I am today, eighty-five years old! I am still as strong today as the day Moses sent me out; I'm just as vigorous to go out to battle now as I was then. Now give me this hill country that the LORD promised me that day. You yourself heard then that the Anakites were there and their cities were large and fortified, but, the LORD helping me, I will drive them out just as he said. (Joshua 14:10-12)

This generation of youth may well be the Joshua Generation, but there is a Caleb Connection out there as well—a generation of youth workers who stands behind the bold, courageous students of the Joshua Generation just as Caleb stood behind Joshua as he led the Israelites into the Promised Land. Let me suggest three ways in which this is true.

First, Caleb was willing to stand alone and believe God's promises, even though circumstances seemed to suggest otherwise. Today's youth culture is in many ways a train wreck; it doesn't make sense that dynamic spiritual leaders would rise out of this wreckage. Youth today bring with them a tremendous amount of personal baggage from broken families, abuse and the like. They are busier than ever with school, sports and other extracurriculars, as well as jobs. The survey folks tell us that Christian students aren't, by and large, much different. But many youth workers believe that radically committed spiritual leadership *is* emerging out of this "train wreck" generation, and they are doing what they can to identify and empower these upcoming leaders.

Second, Caleb was willing to take a back seat to the emerging leadership and simply serve. Joshua got all the ink; his name made the headlines. There is no book of Caleb, even though he was the guy that spoke up first. But the fact that he reemerges in Joshua 14 shows us that even though he didn't get all the credit that Joshua did, he hung in there and fought alongside his countrymen. I suppose he could have just kicked back and waited for his promised inheritance (Numbers 14:24). But apparently he didn't go into early retirement and get himself an RV to cruise through Sinai and Canaan.

Caleb-style youth workers are ones who adjust with the times, realizing that the spotlight doesn't always need to be on them in order for their ministry to be "successful." Caleb-style youth workers let a student give the message at youth group, knowing full well that they could have done a much better job. But they also know that with some encouragement and mentoring, that student will soon leave them in the dust in terms of spiritual power and the ability to be heard by peers—the latter likely being the case already.

*COME ON, ADMIT IT—THOSE ALL-NIGHTERS ARE A LITTLE HARDER TO RECOVER FROM THESE DAYS.

Finally, even in his old age, Caleb was more than ready and willing to go after the big guys and possess his inheritance. Age had not diminished his physical prowess or his courageous, passionate faith. While it is true that "maturing" youth workers with young families and diminishing stamina perhaps **can't keep up*** with youth the way they used to, we *can* (and should) continue to grow in passionate, risk-taking faith.

Not too long ago I sat in a coffee shop with one of these emerging leaders of the Joshua Generation. A recent high school graduate, he has a growing national platform and speaks with authority to his generation. I am older than his dad and have been doing youth ministry since well before he was born. I am also well aware that it is people like this young man who are going to lead his generation into possession of their inheritance. I have met an increasing number of them in recent years.

Caleb types hang in there doing youth ministry because we believe that some day soon, God will raise up young leaders such as this guy. Now is our time to empower them, take a back seat and supporting role to their emerging leadership yet *not* disengage and slide into early retirement. There are still Anakites out there that need a thrashing.

I have no plans to retire from this youth ministry gig. I am far too old to qualify for the Joshua Generation, but I want to be a part of the Caleb Connection. My prayer is that my spiritual passion would be as aflame during my "mature" years as it was when I was in my late teens and early twenties, and that my passion would inspire emerging student leaders. We desperately need Christians among the older generations to act as Calebs, refusing to cruise into spiritual retirement but, instead, finishing well with a blaze of spiritual glory.

I can hear that old geezer Caleb's cry echoing through the millennia: *"Give me this hill!"*

THIRD
MOVEMENT

RESTORING
OUR UNITY

NINE

"WE ARE ONE"

The Mandate of Love and Unity

---

u•ni•ty (yōo'nĭ-tē)

1. The state or quality of being one; singleness.
2. The state or quality of being in accord; harmony.
3. The combination or arrangement of parts into a whole; unification.
4. Singleness or constancy of purpose or action; continuity.

Let's revisit a question posed earlier in the book: What would it take to fulfill the Great Commission among emerging generations of students? Or, on a slightly smaller scale, what would it take to give every young person in a community the opportunity to grapple with the gospel? Is that actually possible?

I believe so.* And many of the issues I covered elsewhere in this book—personal holiness and obedience, spiritual warfare, strategic prayer—are vital factors in bringing this about. But there is one additional, critical factor that must be addressed.

*I'VE READ THE END OF THE BOOK. WE WIN.

If the body of Christ is to fulfill its mission on earth, the enmity that has traditionally existed among denominations, organizations and local bodies in a shared geographical region must be put to a stop. When Jesus gives his final marching orders to his disciples (John 13—17, often called the Upper Room Discourse) he bookends his comments with two imperatives. The first is a call to love one another: "By this all men will know that you are my disciples, if you love one another" (John 13:35). The second is a prayer for unity: "May they be brought to complete unity to let the world know that you sent me and have loved them even as you have loved me"(John 17:23). Jesus tells his disciples, and us, that our greatest apologetic will not be a well-articulated gospel message or quality programming or a comprehensive missions thrust but rather how well we get along with each other. You see, love and unity are a *really big deal* to God.

One of the reasons God cares so much about love and unity is that they are reflections of the character of the Trinity. Among all the unfathomable truths about the Triune God, a few are clear: the Father, Son and Holy Spirit are consumed by, and define for us, true love and unity. "Dear friends, let us love one another, for love comes from God. Everyone who loves has been born of God and knows God. Whoever does not love does not know God, because God is love" (1 John 4:7-8). "Hear O Israel: the Lord our God, the Lord is one" (Deuteronomy 6:4).

As we demonstrate love and unity, we reflect the character of the Trinity to the world. And we validate Christ as the Son of God. As Chuck Colson observes:

> The message is clear. The world isn't looking at our tracts and rallies and telecasts and study manuals. It is looking at us and how we behave. When it fails to see the unity of Jesus' followers—the church—it fails to see the validation that Christ is indeed the Son of the living God.[1]

Colson's observation is true in Christendom in general, and also in youth ministry, where students are watching Christian peers and youth workers *very* carefully to see if there is, indeed, any difference in how we live.

The fact that love and unity are a really big deal to God is further demonstrated by Satan's relentless attempts to distort, corrupt and pollute the church's demonstration of love and unity, as seen in denominationalism, theological strife and the like. The church has seemingly spent much of the past two thousand years demonstrating to the world everything *but* love and unity. Obviously that is not entirely true, because the church is still around and doing quite well in many places, thank you very much. But if you were to stop the average un-churched Joe on the road and ask him what comes to mind when you say "Christian church," unfortunately he's likely to respond with comments like "irrelevance," "prudish legalism," or "TV evangelist scandals." We have not always portrayed a very accurate picture to the unbelieving world of what the Bride of Christ should be like.

So how do we get love and unity back in the church? And how do we capitalize on that love and unity to, in the words of Joe Aldrich, "start and sustain a movement of God in a community"? Do we drop all our denominational and organizational affiliations, and become one big homogenous church? I don't think so. The development of an environment in which love and unity are displayed doesn't require us all to be alike or to sign a mutual covenant or to belong to the same organization. What it does require is a working understanding of our union both with Christ (John 14:20) and with one another in Christ (1 Corinthians 12:12, 17). Aldrich notes:

> Unity is not unanimity. Nor is it uniformity. When there is a lot of pressure for uniformity, we don't have unity. When we have true unity, we don't all have to be the same. Furthermore, unity is not union. God has not called

us into some kind of structural or organizational union. Paul's command is that we keep (not make) the unity that we already have because of our union with Christ.[2]

If loving unity is not unanimity or uniformity, then what is it? The best illustration I can come up with has to do with the process of **making wine.*** Simply put, the process begins when a bunch of grapes are smashed together until their skins burst and the inner juices are allowed to flow together. And similarly, as members of the body of Christ in a particular community, when we position ourselves together to allow the Holy Spirit to break down our "skins,"

*I'VE NEVER MADE WINE, OF COURSE, BUT I'VE HEARD ABOUT HOW IT'S DONE.

then the new wine flows and those in the community who taste it respond, "Hey, this is great stuff!"

Relationships are essential in the development of unity. They are the context in which love and unity are defined and explored, for it is in relationships that trust is established between brothers and sisters in Christ, no matter what denominational or nonessential theological differences may be present. (When we get to heaven, we're likely going to be wrong about *some* nonessential doctrine. Let's argue about it then.) When trust is established in an environment of love and unity, when the walls start to come down between us, we have new freedom to be honest with ourselves and with each other, and the Holy Spirit is able to intensify the process of breaking down our "skins."

And what are these skins? All the junk that keeps us from being clean before God and right with one another: secret sins, prejudices, wrong attitudes, potentially fatal flaws, personal agendas, selfishness and so on—the kind of stuff that fails to attract the blessing of God in our personal lives and ministries, and in our efforts to be light and salt in our communities. So how do we develop an environment of trust necessary to break through these walls?

Corporate Repentance and Reconciliation

Repentance and reconciliation are vital when it comes to developing love and unity among believers. Second Chronicles 7:14 says, "If my people, who are called by my name, will humble themselves, and pray and seek my face, and turn from their wicked ways, then I will hear from heaven, and will forgive their sin and heal their land." Personal humility, prayer, repentance and holiness are all vital to this healing process. But they are crucial on a corporate level as well. I have always appreciated the models of three Old Testament heroes of the faith—Daniel, Ezra and Nehemiah—who dealt with all these issues on a personal level. Yet we also find them in Scripture engaging in humble repentance on behalf of their people and their nations (see Daniel 9:4-20; Ezra 9:5—10:2; Nehemiah 1:4-11). Why? International prayer and reconciliation leader Cindy Jacobs explains:

> Daniel understood about praying and asking for forgiveness for corporate sin. . . . What did Daniel do so God would release the people? He repented on their behalf, by admonishing, "We have sinned and committed iniquity" (see v. 5). This kind of praying was also done by Ezra and Nehemiah and is called "identificational repentance." Identificational repentance occurs when a person repents for the corporate sin of his or her nation. Does that mean

that each person is not personally responsible before God for his or her own individual sins? Of course not. Each person must come to Christ for his or her own sins (see John 3:16; Rev. 20:13). However, corporate sin allows Satan to blind the eyes of whole nations, according to 2 Corinthians 4:4: "Whose minds the god of this age has blinded, who do not believe, lest the light of the gospel of the glory of Christ, who is the image of God, should shine on them."[3]

John Dawson is one of the pioneers of this new Spirit-inspired trend. He comments on Nehemiah's identificational repentance: "What was true in Nehemiah's day is true today. A repentant church, confessing the sins of the nation before God, is America's only hope."[4] Primarily through his International Reconciliation Coalition, he has led the way in pursuing identificational repentance and reconciliation not only between nations but also between racial and ethnic groups.

Reconciliation is a trendy topic in secular circles today as more and more people realize emotions in our melting-pot country are going to boil over unless we find solutions to the racial and ethnic tensions that permeate almost every level of society. Attempting reconciliation through open dialogue and mediation is a positive step, but the Bible makes clear that a key starting point in the reconciliation process is repentance—and repentance is *not* a trendy topic in secular circles today! However, we who through repentance have been reconciled to God are charged to be his messengers of reconciliation (2 Corinthians 5:17-21). This includes both vertical reconciliation (between us and God) and the horizontal reconciliation (between each another; Ephesians 2:14-18).

So how does this all relate to youth ministry? As those who

minister among what is perhaps the most racially and ethnically diverse generation our nation has ever seen, we need to be leaders in delivering the reconciliation message of the cross and helping youth (as well as others) be reconciled to one another. In *Healing America's Wounds* Dawson addresses not only ethnic and racial reconciliation (primarily African American and Native American issues) but also the need for sexual and political reconciliation in our polarized country. Could generational reconciliation also fit in the mix? For example, is there a place for a generation such as the Baby Boomers to repent of the legacy of selfishness they have passed on to their children? Would that make a difference? The last verse of the Old Testament indicates that it would: "He will turn the hearts of the fathers to their children, and the hearts of the children to their fathers; or else I will come and strike the land with a curse" (Malachi 4:6).

Repentance and reconciliation are usually long and challenging journeys for all parties concerned. And they are, indeed, a *process*. Not long ago I was standing with a small group of fellow youth workers in Birmingham, Alabama. Directly **in front of us*** was the 16th Street Baptist Church, where in 1963 four schoolgirls were killed when a racist's bomb went off in the building. Across the street to our right was Kelly Ingram (formerly West) Park, the site of a protest march led by Dr. Martin Luther King, to which the police responded with fire hoses, attack dogs and multiple arrests. Behind us was the Birmingham Civil Rights Institute, which chronicles in brutal detail both the travesties of the past and the progress (although limited) that

*THAT IS ONE INTENSE STREET CORNER!

has been made over the past few decades.

Our group that day included an African American youth worker from Birmingham. It was obvious that this guy had logged a few more laps around the track of life than the rest of us, but what really caught our attention was when he said, "I was here in 1963 and marched with Dr. King." Once the hair standing up on our arms laid back down, we heard a first-person account of what really went on in the city during that turbulent season which so impacted the rest of our country. Later, I asked if he felt that much progress had been made in the area of repentance for the many atrocities of the past. His response was telling: "You know, I'm getting a little tired of white folks groveling at my feet. It's time to move beyond repenting for the past, and on to healing for the future." Well said. Repentance is the necessary first step, but it is one step of many.

One of the most effective methods for cultivating trust and transparency in my own life is attending prayer summits with fellow youth workers. Basically, a prayer summit is a group of youth workers from a community going away together for an extended period of time, with no keynote speakers, no special music, no seminars and no agenda except to seek the Lord and inquire of him—together. It's a multiday corporate prayer retreat. Does that sound scary? It is; but it is life-changing for the participants and one of the better ways I know of to build corporate unity.

These prayer summits can be pretty intense affairs. The worship is generally a capella, though youth workers sometimes bring guitars, and Scripture and prayer are liberally laced into the mixture. Men and women spill their guts before God and before one another. But it's not just an airing of dirty laundry; people come clean before God and before one another; the body takes over and does what it is supposed to do (ministering to one another), and tremendous healing takes place. At some summits the confession time takes days. Other times participants end up on their faces before the Lord, awestruck by his majesty and power. Tears flow freely; Communion becomes a time of treading on holy ground. And through it all, God shows us that we are all sinners, saved by grace, and that we desperately need each other.

In my city's youth ministry movement, the members of the servant-leadership team are not just colaborers; many of us have been through years of prayer summits/retreats[5] together. We represent varied denominational backgrounds and ministry styles, yet **I would trust any of them***

✳I HOPE
THE REVERSE
IS
TRUE!

to speak at one of my seminars or teach students on my behalf. We are genuinely more concerned about reaching the students in our city than we are about building our own little ministry kingdoms. We have prayed together, played together, rejoiced together and wept together. And we would all parrot the words of Aldrich, who states:

> In this movement we're watching, there is a desire to see God really impact a community. But to impact a community, we must be a community. To be a community we must have unity. To have unity we must have humility. And to have humility we must rediscover holiness.[6]

By no means have all the youth workers in our city attended a prayer summit, but something similar takes place at a local level. Across the city, youth workers who are in geographical proximity gather on a monthly basis to share their lives, minister to one another and intercede for kids within their mission field.

At a recent gathering I attended, there were eight or ten of us sprawled out on the hand-me-down couches that furnish many church youth rooms. Posters on the walls, a drum set in the corner, and photos of kids on the bulletin board completed the look. A half-dozen local churches and a handful of youth ministry organizations were represented—men and women who share a common passion (kids), vocation (youth ministry), mission field (the community and schools in their area) and DNA (I call it "youth worker wacko"). We gathered to pray, share our stories, encourage one another and bear one another's burdens.

John shared about his recent trip to India—twenty-four days with a team of evangelists, sharing the good news of the gospel of Jesus with literally hundreds of thousands of spiritually hungry people who worship a myriad of Hindu gods. In one city, John related, cool butter is sold in front of an idol of a local deity. Penitents purchase the butter and throw it at the idol to "cool him down" and thus appease him. Fear and hopelessness permeate the culture—too much sin and you might be reincarnated as a cockroach.

Kent's story featured him in a store that sells "lingerie" to questionable clients, if you get the drift, trying to minister to a belligerent mom whose daughter had just given her life to Christ. He shared how God repeatedly gave him just the right responses to the outbursts of profanity and jeering questions, disarming this lady in a way that only God could orchestrate and beginning to remove the spiritual blindness that kept her from responding to the wooing of the Lover of her soul.

Miles, a junior high pastor, was struggling with the implications of an influx of close to eighty unchurched kids into his youth group. Of course he was elated they were coming, but he was quite transparent about the accompanying challenges: kids using expletives to describe their sin; discomfort on the part of students who grew up in the church (and their parents); adult volunteers who couldn't (or wouldn't) deal with it and were quitting. Then Miles dropped the bomb: "And my wife has cancer. Stage four."

Questions followed; he went on to describe the nature of the cancer, how he and his wife were dealing with it, and the prophetic words he had received concerning her healing that gave him great encouragement, hope and faith. The others there offered compassion, empathy and deep, heartfelt prayers of faith for their brother and his wife who were in great need. As I walked to my car later I was reminded once again of the value in being spiritually real with my colaborers; it beats planning events (as important as they are) any time.

Working Around the Differences

Our united, citywide youth ministry movement is still a work in progress when it comes to that holiness-humility-unity-community-impact progression described by Dr. Aldrich. For example, not getting hung up on nonessential doctrine sounds good in a book, but in practice it sometimes takes a bit of work to flesh that out in practical terms. In our united prayer times, both charismatic and noncharismatic streams are usually represented. Some participants like to pray in tongues; others have a real problem with that. So what do we do when we're praying together? Because we've learned to love and trust each other in the context of personal relationships, both sides have given preference to the other. People pray in tongues under their breath so as not to draw attention to their praying, and those who don't pray in tongues give them the freedom and space to do so.

Since we're a work in progress, we're in no hurry to rush ahead of God. As he humbles us by breaking down walls, and as we begin to rediscover his holiness, we begin to be renewed *together*. And we become convinced *together* that our responsibility is to seek God's face before we seek his hand. I mentioned this earlier, but it bears repeating: youth workers have the tendency to make plans, then ask God to bless them. And so in our summits we focus on seeking the face of God together and trust that in his timing he will reveal to us a divine strategy for fulfilling the Great Commission among students in our community.

What might that strategy be? At this point I can only speculate. However, the path we are walking today is different from many strategies we have tried before. In the past our strategy was built around large, multi-church rallies or citywide evangelistic thrusts in which we were all drawn together for a common cause. Operational unity surfaced so that we could pull the event off, and frequently we saw a wonderful harvest. But what happened after the event? Usually we crawled back into our ministry foxholes to once again pursue our own agendas, and it was business as usual. Conversely, our citywide movement today is rooted in prayer and relationship, not events. It is driven by the desire to see real, live, biblical love and unity surface and remain among us as we rediscover God's holiness together. Events are only part of that process; when loving unity is in full bloom we do not crawl back in our holes when the events are concluded. That is a critical distinction.

Prayer summits do not have the corner on the market in terms of corporate renewal. But they are a wonderful model of what God desires to do in and through his people if we give him the freedom to do so.

Let me ask you a few questions:

- What do you think would happen in your community if

all the youth workers were to come together on a regular basis, not primarily to plan events, but for the purpose of seeking the Lord and developing unity?

- What would happen if you humbled yourselves, **"came clean"*** in front of your peers and experienced from them complete acceptance and unconditional love?

- What would happen if the denominational, organizational, ethnic, gender, generational and relational walls in your community were to come crashing down?

- What would happen if you together rediscovered God's holiness in a way that left you all face down on the floor, speechless? I have experienced this, and it is *epic*.

∗SCARY THOUGHT!

- What would happen if all of you, or at least a critical mass, experienced and incarnated true biblical love and unity? Don't you think that would look awfully attractive to kids in your community who have never experienced anything remotely close to that kind of love and unity? And don't you think God might want to do something through you that is bigger than your wildest dreams in order to reach students in your community?

I think so.

TEN

"WE ARE ASKING"
The Power of United Prayer

ask (ăsk)

1. To put a question to.
2. To make a request of or for.
3. To make inquiry; seek information.
4. To make a request; seek an answer.

Asignificant part of my ministry in recent years has been devoted to mobilizing united prayer. Because there aren't a whole lot of us doing that in youth ministry, I have, in certain circles, been tagged with the moniker "Prayer Boy." At my age, being called a boy is a compliment, but I have always been uncomfortable with the label; people often assume that because I mobilize prayer, I must be a big-league intercessor. And I'm not.

Intercession is not listed in Scripture as a spiritual gift, but it's clear that God has given certain people the ability to engage in prayer in extraordinary ways. Some of the intercessors I know get up in the wee hours of the morning, head for their prayer closet and emerge several hours later with tear-stained cheeks. They have just prayed for most of the known world, and done so with power and accuracy.

Well, I'm not wired that way. Early morning hours in my prayer closet are sometimes called a nap. And though I wish I could say intercession comes naturally for me, the truth is that my commitment to intercession is one that must be renewed daily; it is hard work for me. My mind often wanders from my prayer list to my do-to list.

I'm not trying to excuse my failings in prayer by saying I'm not "gifted" in that area. We are *all* called to be faithful in prayer (Romans 12:12). Being devoted to prayer (1 Corinthians 7:5; Colossians 4:2) and praying continually (1 Thessalonians 5:17—quite a concept) are not optional. And we are *all* called to be clear-minded and self-controlled in our praying (1 Peter 4:7), which is where the discipline comes into play. So, I continue to persevere at personal prayer, knowing that even if I don't transform into a closet warrior, my seasons of intimate communion with the Father will increase in quantity and quality. He will hear my prayers just as clearly as he hears those of the closet intercessors.

That said, I have discovered an arena of prayer where I *can* be involved at a big-league level: united prayer. Jesus made it clear that corporate prayer packs some unusual power: "Again, I tell you that if two of you on earth agree about anything you ask for, it will be done for you by my Father in heaven. For where two or three come together in my name, there am I with them" (Matthew 18:19-20). The early church certainly put his teaching into practice. After Jesus' ascension (Acts 1), the small band of disciples "all joined together constantly in prayer" (Acts 1:14). Following Pentecost, the early church was characterized as being devoted to united prayer (Acts 2:42). United prayer was their response to Peter and John's initial run-in with the Sanhedrin (Acts 4:24-30), and Peter's release from Herod's imprisonment was the direct result of united prayer (Acts 12:5-14).

United prayer is not only powerful, it is accessible; it can happen anywhere that two or more can gather, and anyone can do it. This type of prayer illustrates the beauty of Paul's body metaphor in 1 Corinthians 12: neophyte and seasoned intercessors, those who are comfortable praying out loud and those who have rarely done so, can all agree together in prayer. The power in united prayer comes not from the eloquence or fervency or theology of those praying but from the coming together of those praying. Such prayer can be a wonderful classroom experience for those wanting to ascend their own prayer learning curve. Veteran international prayer leader Dick Eastman writes:

> Only as we apply our knowledge of prayer to the actual practice of prayer will we discover the practical power of prayer.
>
> Fletcher of Madeley, a fellow worker with John Wesley, illustrates the importance of making prayer practical. This dedicated warrior had a most unusual conclusion to many of his lectures. Often, after discussing themes on prayer and spiritual growth, Fletcher would say to his students, "That is the theory; now will those who want the practice come along up to my room."
>
> Often all of Fletcher's students would quietly follow this godly saint to his room for one or two hours of actual practice in the art of prayer. They knew the secret was in "doing," not merely in "knowing."[1]

I have already discussed at length the power of united prayer among youth workers in a Prayer summit. Let me mention three other forms of united prayer that are especially relevant to youth ministry.

Prayerwalking

Most of us struggle in our prayer lives with alertness and focus; our minds are prone to wander, we get drowsy, we lose our concentration. Students have the same struggles, and they are compounded by the fact that many (perhaps most) of them have a very difficult time sitting still! Prayerwalking is a wonderful, effective alternative for anyone who has such struggles, and it can provide a tremendous boost to the prayer efforts of most people.

Steve Hawthorne and Graham Kendrick define *prayerwalking* as "praying on-site with insight." They describe a trend that is quickly spreading:

> Across the globe God is stirring ordinary believers to pray persistently while walking their cities street by street. Some use rather well-arranged plans. Others flow with Spirit-given prompts. Their prayers run the gamut from lofty appeals to pinpoint petitions, ranging beyond their own homes to their neighborhoods. It's hard to stop there, so most of them eventually burst into prayers for the entire campus or city or nation. No quick fix is envisioned. But expectancy seems to expand with every mile. Most of these pray-ers don't imagine themselves to be just bravely holding flickering candles toward an overwhelming darkness. Rather, long fuses are being lit for anticipated explosions of God's love.[2]

Such a Spirit-driven trend seems to be tailor-made for students! In fact, youth workers and students are taking up prayerwalking in fast-increasing numbers. Some examples:

- In Austin, Texas, students from several different youth groups gathered to march around the perimeter of a local high school singing praise songs. They then broke up into smaller groups to continue walking and praying for the school.

- On a September morning each year, millions of students gather at their schools for See You at the Pole, a "modified" prayerwalk.
- In Portland, Oregon, members of a church youth group met with leaders of a ministry to street kids and walked the streets of downtown Portland praying for those kids.
- Youth groups around the country are engaging in "Jericho walks," where they march around school campuses, claiming them for Christ.

Prayerwalking provides several obvious benefits: (1) it keeps participants alert; (2) it gives them a visual reminder of the object of their prayers; (3) it has an aggressive quality that motivates students; (4) it is fun!

On-Site Prayer

People in youth ministry are recognizing more and more the crucial role of intercession in youth activities, especially larger outreach events, when the battle becomes heated for the souls of those in attendance. Many of these events now have intercessors pray through buildings before students arrive and remain on site in another room, praying fervently during the event.

One of my first experiences of on-site prayer was at a Portland evangelistic rally attended by around 5,500 students. I was part of a team of seven intercessors who assembled a few hours before the rally began. In that time we prayed around the perimeter of the facility, asking God to place a hedge of protection around the building, and we prayed on the stage and through the seating area. When the rally began, we moved to a prayer room and continued to intercede, inviting God's presence, asking for his protection, and praying that his power would work mightily through the music, the testimonies and the invitation. Our prayer time included "reconnaissance" trips into the auditorium to pray for students and get further direction from the Lord for our prayers.

During one of our "reconnaissance" excursions, two women reported that they had sensed an oppressive, occultic spirit over one particular section in the crowd, and had accordingly prayed very aggressively over that particular group of students. Later, as the evening wound down, these two approached me with big grins on their faces and a young man in tow. As it turns out, the student had ties to the occult, but he had been touched by the Spirit of God that evening and wanted to be

*JUST A COINCIDENCE? I DON'T THINK SO.

delivered from bondage. As we asked him what section he had been sitting in, **we already knew the answer.***

Soon the tranquillity of our prayer room was shattered by the sound of doors slamming open; over seven hundred students who had just been "rescued from the kingdom of darkness and brought . . . into the kingdom of the Son" (Colossians 1:13) streamed in! As youth workers scrambled to do the essential follow-up with so many new believers, our team continued to pray over these new converts as we rejoiced with the angels in heaven.

In the ensuing years, I have been involved in scores of on-site prayer initiatives for events both small and large. I have led teams of adults who have interceded (in a variety of creative ways) for ten to twelve hours a day over the course of a five-day event. I have also led students in prayer coverage for an outreach event targeting their peers. Participants in these initiatives have ranged from prominent international prayer leaders to intimidated new believers. Many were significantly stretched by their involvement, and most have found the united-prayer experience to be wonderful.

Youth-Worker Network Gatherings

In my hometown of Portland, youth worker networking has been taking place for well over twenty years. Historically, it was centered around a specific purpose or event: a training conference or outreach we do together, or a Billy Graham or Luis Palau event. As a result, participation ebbed and flowed. Before, during and immediately after the event, involvement was high, but it wasn't sustained over the long haul. When there was no event-oriented reason for coming together, attendance would flag.

After the 1992 Billy Graham Crusade, those of us who comprised the youth committee acknowledged the unprecedented breadth of representation on that committee and decided that we needed to keep coming together. As we prayerfully processed what our meetings would look like in the future, we made several conscious decisions:

1. Our networking would be primarily prayer- and relationship-driven.

2. Enduring relationships would take precedence over ministry-strategy development and event planning.

3. Strategy and events would flow out of united prayer as we together sought the Lord and inquired of him.

4. Our first, foremost and prevailing strategy for reaching the youth of our city would be to mobilize and deploy unprecedented united prayer.

A decade later, a handful of monthly regional youth-worker network meetings has grown to nine, and involvement has grown from dozens to hundreds of youth workers—male and female, vocational and volunteer, charismatic and conservative, urban and suburban, bright-eyed rookies and grizzled veterans. Wonderful events have grown out of many of these gatherings, but they all remain foundationally prayer-driven and prayer-focused. Tears are shed, burdens are borne, and the blessing of God (see Psalm 133) is evident in many ways.

Postscript: The Prayer Life of the Youth Leader

Even the most cursory examination of the great men and women of the Bible reveals a gaping chasm between their prayer lives and what passes for prayer in the lives of many, if not most, Western Christians. The heroes of the faith found in the Scriptures were by no means flawless; many had profound struggles with sin issues both great and small. But their lives were in most instances characterized by the mandate in 1 Thessalonians 5:17 to "pray continually," one we so often try to trivialize or rationalize.

Christians in other parts of the world seem to take the biblical examples and admonitions concerning prayer much more seriously than most Americans. Argentinian believers gather by the tens of thousands for all-night prayer rallies, and Korean Christians spend an average of two to three hours daily in closet-style prayer. Conversely, surveys tell us that American clergy spend, on average, seven minutes a day in prayer. Likely their congregations average even less. With such a profound discrepancy between the biblical pattern and the actual practice of prayer on the part of so many Western believers, dare we wonder why revival tarries in our countries?

I am not aware of any survey that has measured the prayer lives of youth workers, but I have my suspicions that we are somewhat closer to the American clergy average than we are to contemporary prayer warriors. But if we want to be used by God to reach students, our prayer lives must change. Here are a few practical tips:

- If you are not in an accountability group, join one immediately. Make prayer an integral part of your meeting, and have your group hold you accountable for certain prayer standards.

- Find prayer warriors in your area, and hang out with them when they are praying. If you can find someone who will mentor you in prayer, go for it!

- Read stuff on prayer. There is no shortage of insightful, inspirational, motivational and downright practical material on the topic. Even biographies of great prayer warriors can be helpful, but resist the temptation to put these people on a pedestal; they are human, and flawed too.

- Add a little more overt praise and worship to your music listening list.

- Find the intercessor groups in your community, and hang with them as well. This will sharpen your own prayer life, and it will also provide great insight into what God is doing in your community; he often speaks to intercessors ahead of time so their prayers will be on target.

I am convinced that the greatest way youth workers can affect the lives of students is by diligently praying for them. There are a number of ways to make intercession both practical (so it would pack the most spiritual bang) and creative (so we will be more likely to stick with it over the long haul). For example, one of my biggest struggles as a youth pastor was learning and remembering the names of students. So I started packing a Polaroid camera with me and taking pictures of students. I had them write their name and school on the little white strip at the bottom of the Polaroids and then used them as memory flash cards.

Then I realized that these same flash cards could serve as prayer reminders for each student in my ministry! As I turned to each card, I would mentally sort through what I knew about that particular student and how I could most effectively pray for him or her. That, in turn, led me to begin calling students to ask for relevant prayer requests from them. I didn't call to invite them to a youth activity or to query why they weren't in Sunday school (as they might expect), but just to ask how I might pray more accurately for them. That I would call just to ask for prayer requests, without any ulterior motive, was nearly as great a ministry to the students as actually praying for them!

The following are a few more ideas:

- For just a few bucks, you can pick up a computer program designed to remind you of upcoming birthdays. The program can be modified so that you are prompted to pray for specific students every time you turn your computer on.

- Send students a postcard to let them know you are praying for them.

- Let parents know that you are praying for their son or daughter, and ask them for insights that will help you focus your prayers. Communicate to them your desire to pray with them for their children and for them as parents.

- Put up a "Weekly Prayer Focus" bulletin board in your youth room at church; put up pictures of featured students so that others in your group can join in praying for them.

*I CALL THIS "CYBER-PRAYER."

- Make your e-mail address available to students and parents so they can send you prayer requests and praise reports, and **send students e-mail prayers.*** If you are really into computers or the Internet, post your own website or develop your own bulletin board for prayer.

- Model prayer for students. Prayer is not taught; like most vital spiritual disciplines, it is caught. When you meet with a small group, don't relegate prayer to the last five hurried minutes of your gathering.

ELEVEN

"WE ARE LISTENING"

The Importance of Discernment

---

dis•cern (dĭ-sûrn′, -zûrn′)

1. To perceive with the eyes or intellect; detect.
2. To recognize or comprehend mentally.
3. To perceive or recognize as being different or distinct; distinguish.

The . . . men of Issachar . . . understood the times and knew what Israel should do. (1 Chronicles 12:23, 32)

. . .

Think globally, act locally" is a slogan used widely by environmentalists to challenge people to consider the global environmental implications of their actions and adjust them accordingly on a local level. For example, one might take into consideration the implications that driving a gas-guzzling car or lawn mower has for global warming, and then choose to buy a smaller, more efficient car or a **push mower.***

The credo also has significant application for considering contemporary ministry strategies, especially in a day when God is "on the move" around the world in exciting ways. Even the casual observer of current missiology can see that the Holy Spirit is giving people new

*WATCH FOR A RUSH AMONG YOUTH WORKERS TO BUY PUSH MOWERS.

paradigms for effective ministry in many parts of the world. Tremendous spiritual harvests are taking place in countries such as Argentina, Korea, China and Russia. Unprecedented cooperation has allowed the gospel to penetrate beyond the former Iron Curtain with great effectiveness. Movements of prayer are exploding across our country and world. Terms such as "spiritual mapping," and "strategic intercession" are fast becoming buzzwords of a new way of fulfilling the Great Commission.

These new paradigms have a very direct and relevant application to contemporary youth ministry. A strategic dimension of youth ministry renewal is to "think globally"—to understand what God is doing in various parts of the world—and to "act locally"—to apply those principles to youth work at the grassroots level. Just as Jesus admonished the seven churches in Revelation 2:7, "He who has an ear, let him hear what the Spirit says," so should youth workers hear with discernment what the Spirit is saying to the church today, and respond accordingly.

In a time when culture and technology are changing at a whirlwind pace, youth workers need to recognize the movement of Holy Spirit as well. The paradigms or strategies that were relevant twenty, ten or even five years ago are likely not relevant any longer. For example, in 1990 Gordon Aeschliman, former editor of *World Christian* magazine, described ten current paradigm shifts in his book *Global Trends: Ten Changes Affecting Christians Everywhere*. His list includes the following items:

1. The Shrinking Globe (through transportation, communication, economic advances)
2. The Islamic Revolution

3. Reaching the World's Poor

4. The Earth Groans (environmentalism)

5. Setting the Captive Free (the world democratic revolution)

6. The Urban Challenge (population migration from rural to urban settings)

7. The Gorbachev Revolution (decline of communism in the Soviet Union)

8. The Fading Glory of the West

9. The Evangelism Crisis (lack of progress in spreading the Gospel)

10. The Internationalization of the Gospel[1]

In 2001 Robert Stearns wrote a similar book titled *Prepare the Way: Twelve Spiritual Signposts for the New Millennium.* His list has some similarities to that of Aeschliman but also shows some significant additions:

1. Passion for Jesus: having "an earnest, abandoned passion for Jesus and little or no tolerance for lifeless religion"

2. Ears to Hear: "rediscovering the need and joy of hearing the voice of the Lord"

3. Global Relevance and Release: "uniquely equipped and mobilized for cross-cultural evangelism at home and abroad"

4. Living Stones: "relationally driven"

5. Creativity Unleashed: "fully released in the power of creativity"

6. One Body, Diverse Members: "intentional in reconciliation"

7. Spiritual Authority: "a mature understanding of spiritual warfare"

8. The Citywide Family of God: "embrac[ing] the concept of the City Church"

9. Abiding in the Secret Place: "embrac[ing] the value of the quiet place"

10. A Heart for the Poor: "not just to giv[ing] to the poor, but . . . be[ing] in relationship with the poor"

11. Restoring the Tabernacle of David: "abandoned in worship"

12. Israel: "understand more fully the uniqueness of Israel in the plans and purposes of the Lord"[2]

Not to be outdone by these guys, I composed my own youth worker-friendly **list*** of trends in a monograph I wrote in 1996 for the National Network of Youth Ministries:

*SORRY ABOUT ALL THESE LISTS.

1. United Prayer

2. Spiritual Warfare

3. Spiritual Mapping

4. Strategic Intercession

5. Identificational Repentance and Reconciliation

6. Citywide Strategies[3]

Not surprisingly, the lists vary greatly. My list today is different from the earlier one I wrote that's listed above. By the time this book gets to print my list may have changed again! And though I develop in this book several of the newer paradigms relevant to youth ministry, the point is not that we need to jump on the bandwagon and implement the most current paradigms. Rather, we each need to seek the Lord and discern what the Spirit seems to be saying to us individually and inquire of him as to what is applicable to our own situation.

It's important to understand that spiritual paradigms and cultural trends are very different animals. There are a number of trends, such as postmodernism, nonlinear thinking and the Internet explosion, that we must be aware of and responsive to as youth workers, but these are different from the paradigms the Spirit gives to the church. The former are culturally generated; the latter, Spirit-initiated. Youth workers must become Spirit analysts as well as cultural analysts.

The Church in the City

In 1989 John Dawson, international director of urban missions for Youth with a Mission (YWAM), penned the visionary *Taking Our Cities for God*. A practical textbook on targeting entire cities for Christ, it draws heavily on Dawson's experiences ministering in Los Angeles around the 1984 Summer Olympics. The book is pioneering in the way it weaves elements such as spiritual mapping, strategic intercession, tactical prayer and strategic cooperation into a cohesive plan for citywide evangelism.

In the years since Dawson's book was first published, citywide evangelistic strategies have begun to spring up everywhere, both in the United States and overseas. Over fifty cities were represented at the 1993 A.D. 2000 Consultation on City Strategies, and developing city models from Pittsburgh, New York, Atlanta, the Twin Cities and Portland were presented. As of 2002, Mission America's City Impact Roundtable has identified scores of additional citywide movements. These models are all paradigms given to the body in various places as answers to the question, "What does it take to sustain a movement of God in a particular geographical location?"

In Portland, dramatic results among youth at the 1992 Billy Graham Crusade convinced youth workers in the city of the benefits of strategic cooperation. Momentum from the Crusade led to the development of the Portland Youth Foundation, which involves close to four hundred vocational youth workers in a variety of relational gatherings, prayer focuses and large catalytic events. In Wichita, youth ministries throughout the city organized Youth Crisis Awareness Week, involving seventy-three school assemblies, a rally that attracted nearly fifteen thousand young people and a variety of other gatherings. Over four thousand students made decisions for Christ. Youth ministry city strategies are developing in many other cities* around the country as well.

*NO OFFENSE TO RURAL YOUTH MINISTRY, BUT

MOST YOUTH LIVE IN METROPOLITAN AREAS.

The challenge for youth leaders ministering in the city is to be willing to subordinate their own personal ministry agendas for the greater cause of Christ, and to spiritually link arms with others in their cities to develop a Spirit-led, comprehensive strategy for reaching the entire student community with the claims of Christ.

Spiritual Mapping

The term "spiritual mapping" first surfaced in print in the 1991 book *The Last of the Giants* by missiologist George Otis. He defines it as an attempt "to see our world (or region or city) as it really is, not as it appears to be, . . . superimposing our understanding of forces and events in the spiritual domain onto places and circumstances in the material world."[4]

Spiritual mapping is, in part, an aid in answering questions that have long nagged missiologists: Why are certain geographical areas in the world so difficult to penetrate with the gospel message? Why have vast areas of the Middle East and Asia yielded so little spiritual fruit over the centuries? Why do conventional evangelism strategies fail miserably in these areas? The term has gained familiarity and popularity in many missions circles, and there are several books now available that are devoted to the subject.[5] But the concept has been criticized by some who consider it "extrabiblical" since the phrase "spiritual mapping" isn't found in the **Bible.*** Despite the somewhat new and controversial status of spiritual mapping, the con-

"YOUTH MINISTRY" ISN'T FOUND IN THE BIBLE EITHER.

cept does have application in youth ministry. Ever wonder why some campuses are historically quite open to Christian workers and have significant student-led movements operating, while others seem to be resistant to nearly every effort to penetrate the student community?

In my hometown, most veteran youth workers can easily identify the "open" and "closed" campuses; in many cases the status of the campuses has not changed in decades. One particular inner-city high school has several student-led clubs and groups functioning, and many local churches have ongoing campus ministries there. Just a few miles down the road is another high school with a far different story: no student movements and little, if any, local church contact. Why the difference?

I believe the difference can be attributed to more than just the success of certain youth workers and the effectiveness of dynamic student leaders. A better understanding of the relationship between a community's response to ministry and spiritual warfare may further the cause of Christ at historically "closed" campuses.

Spiritual mapping is linked to spiritual warfare, but it isn't "spiritual ghost-busting." Rather, it is an attempt to better understand the "strongholds" in place in a campus or community in order to pray and evangelize more strategically. Evangelist Ed Silvoso defines a stronghold as "a mind-set impregnated with hopelessness that causes us to accept as unchangeable, situations that we know are contrary to the will of God."[6] Strongholds can be overtly demonic, or they can be economic, political, religious or racial, the latter type of strongholds ultimately being controlled by the former, since "the whole world is under the control of the evil one" (1 John 5:19).

So how can we go about using spiritual mapping to discover these strongholds? Begin with fervent prayer; ask God to open your spiritual eyes to see what is really happening on a campus or in a community. Then do some research. Talk with teachers, administrators, coaches, parents and students to get a feel for the environment both past and present. Talk with other youth workers who have ministered in the area. Take a look at the economic and political climate. Are racial issues prevalent? Do cults or the occult have a presence? As you do your research, are there spiritual "handles" being revealed that you can grab a hold of in focused intercessory prayer?

This might not sound that much different than the traditional methods employed by youth workers trying to penetrate a campus, and it's not. I used to hand out a worksheet with similar questions to my volunteer staff when they were assigned to a campus. At that time, though, they treated the questions with interest but usually did only a cursory job of completing them. We no longer have that luxury.

Let me share one additional story with you. Several years ago a parachurch organization that I work with on occasion was in the process of acquiring 56,000 acres, a pretty significant piece of land! This land included the infrastructure and buildings to house, with some renovation, several thousand student campers and support personnel. The place had world-class youth camp written all over it. It even had its own airport. And the current owner was considering *donating* the parcel to the organization!

That was the good news; the not-as-good news was that one of the former owners was Bhagwan Shree Rajneesh, leader of a hideous, decadent cult in the early 1980s. He had invested tens of million of dollars in building a city in an obscure valley in the middle of nowhere in eastern Oregon, where bad, bad stuff had gone on, well-documented by the news media, before the movement fell apart. Fortunately, a few of the leaders who were spearheading the acquisition process understood the spiritual issues involved. The first few trips our little prayer SWAT teams made to the property gave most of us the creeps: underground escape tunnels; hidden basement rooms used for developing poisons; parapets where armed guards kept watch; lines of garages that housed the Bhagwan's ninety-plus Rolls Royces. And the spiritual climate in the area was *thick*.

God was apparently not real happy with the current status of this property either. Wildfires in the eastern Oregon sagebrush are common, and one broke out on the property. The fire ran along a ridge to the north side of the developed central valley, sparing all the buildings—except one. The Bhagwan had built himself a little palace in a wooded draw, complete with a personal swimming pool and a special room where he would watch videos while taking hits from a spigot of laughing gas located next to his chair. In a wonderful display of control by God, an offshoot of the wildfire dropped down into this draw and literally burnt that shack to the ground.

Today thousands of students meet Jesus at this camp each summer. But if the spiritual dynamics of the property had not been acknowledged and dealt with early on, I doubt there would be a spiritual harvest like the one taking place today.

Strategic Intercession

Discernment is crucial if we want to minister effectively. Yet we will never be able to discern the Spirit's leading without intercession. Like Jehoshaphat, who admitted when facing an overwhelming army that "we do not know what to do" (2 Chronicles 20:12), ever-increasing numbers of believers are coming to the conclusion that status-quo ministry isn't good enough. We haven't been hitting our target. Strategic prayer leader Tom White puts it this way:

> Several nagging questions have at points plagued my first twenty years of Christian service. Why do so many people fail to receive the generous and free gift offered in Jesus Christ? Why do the cults and the occult maintain so strong a grip on seemingly sincere, seeking people? What lies behind the pervasive and persistent bondage that results from family dysfunction, sexual abuse, and compulsive behaviors. . . . Are we missing something? I think so.[7]

The realization that we're falling short of the target has contributed to the growth of a multifaceted prayer movement. David Bryant's Concerts of Prayer movement, the "Praying Through the Window" thrusts and the growing interest in the National Day of Prayer are a few visible streams of this movement. Intercessors for America has been calling our country to prayer and fasting for over thirty years, and is now pursuing a youth emphasis (Youth Interceding for America). The prayer summit movement, with roots in the Pacific Northwest, is now spreading around the world; over one hundred summits are held yearly in our country and overseas. Recently we have seen a sharp increase in large, prayer-oriented gatherings of believers, such as the National Consultation on United Prayer, the National Christian Leaders' Prayer Summit, national and regional prayer and fasting gatherings, and the Global Consultation on Prayer Evangelism, to name just a few.

The prayer movement is growing within youth ministry as well, as evidenced by gatherings like The Call, the Something's Happening U.S.A., See You at the Pole, the proliferation of concerts of prayer in youth groups and the increased prayer orientation of student-led campus clubs. In Portland, an annual youth worker prayer retreat is augmented by regular times of corporate prayer and numerous prayer events involving students. A similar prayer-priority pattern is to be found in many other locales.

As we continue to gather together to seek God in prayer, he will give us new ways of ministering more effectively. By the time you read this book, the new paradigms of today may be old, cracked ones. So it is imperative that we in youth work are continually seeking to discern what the Spirit is saying to the church today, and that we respond accordingly: "He who has an ear, let him hear" (Revelation 2:7).

SELAH

Lead on, O King eternal, the day of march has come;

Henceforth in fields of conquest Thy tents shall be our home.

Through days of preparation Thy grace has made us strong,

And now, O King eternal, we lift our battle song.

Lead on, O King eternal, to lands of deepest night;

We follow where Thou leadest as heralds of the light.

May we to souls immortal Thy Word of life convey

And open heaven's portal through Christ, the truth, the way.

Lead on, O King eternal; we follow not with fears,

For gladness breaks like morning where'er Thy face appears.

Thy cross is lifted o'er us; we journey in its light;

The crown awaits the conquest; lead on, O God of might.

"LEAD ON, O KING ETERNAL"
ERNEST W. SHURTLEFF (1862-1917)

PATIENT, EXPECTANT HOPE

---

hope (hōp)

1. A wish or desire accompanied by confident expectation of its fulfillment.
2. To expect or desire.
3. Trust, confidence.

In my earlier years of youth ministry, I remember hearing a prominent pastor say on a radio broadcast that he didn't see how Christ's return could come any later than the end of the decade. His prediction gave me hope. I remember thinking, *Cool, a few more years of ministry and we're outta here!* That year was 1978; I guess the guy was a little off.

In the ensuing years, there has been a steady stream of end-times prognosticators who have predicted Christ's imminent return. I get a kick out of their predictions, especially when the date comes and goes. But on another level, I don't fault them too much, because end-times predictions have been with the church since its beginning. Although New Testament writers never set dates, their writing gives the feeling that many of them expected Christ's return during their lifetime.

As Christians we are supposed to anticipate Christ's imminent return, even if we don't know the specific date. And time spent waiting for his return develops in us a patient, expectant hope essential for doing youth ministry from the inside out.

The downside of being, shall we say, "experienced" as a youth worker is compensated for by the upside: **spiritual maturity*** and a broader perspective. Part of that upside—the part that keeps us going—is a patient, expectant hope that the stuff addressed in this movement of the Symphony *will* come to pass. That the unity of the church *will* be restored. That what Francis Schaeffer called "the mark of the Christian"—love for one another—*will* once again be on display to the world. That God *will* answer our prayers for the emerging generations of youth.

*WE HOPE!

In the meantime, we will experience inevitable seasons of frustration and discouragement. At times it seems as though some fellow youth workers couldn't care less about taking the time to tear down the barriers that divide us. Just when it seems like the local church and parachurch organizations are finally cooperating, another dispute will surface. And as I wrote earlier, the coming of age of youth ministry is not significantly influencing the emerging generations, at least to the extent that you and I would like. So how does patient, expectant hope fit into this?

As I was putting the final touches on this book, a series of remarkable events unfolded, reminding me that we can have hope in the fact that God is at work, even when we can't see him, and that his timing is perfect.

I have been praying for the salvation of my parents for over thirty years. I grew up in a morally and ethically healthy home, but my parents did not openly profess a faith in Christ. They viewed my decision at age eighteen to follow Christ, and my commitment to vocational youth ministry some five years later, with a mental raised eyebrow. I never felt anything but complete support from them in my choice of career, but I knew that the decision of their firstborn to become a minister must have been something of a surprise. In the ensuing years I shared the gospel message with my folks innumerable times. As time went on, my approach became less confrontational, and our interaction became less of an argument and more of a healthy discussion. I rarely felt that I was making much progress with them, but I kept trying. And I kept praying. For thirty years.

Then one Sunday at church, our pastor preached from Acts 10. I was struck by the description of Cornelius, who is portrayed in the passage as "devout and God-fearing." But Cornelius was still in need of a Savior, which is why, in part, God sent Peter his way. I thought, *That is a description of my mom and dad—devout and God-fearing but with no saving faith in Christ.* I resolved that morning to use that passage the next time I had a chance to talk with my parents about spiritual things.

That afternoon, I got a call from my Mom. Dad was in the hospital to treat the swelling in his legs caused by congestive heart failure. I went up for a visit that night and the next morning with the Acts 10 passage in my mind, waiting for the opportunity to share it with them. While in my Dad's room the following evening, my Mom asked me, out of the blue, a spiritual question; I took it as an invitation and steered the conversation in a spiritual direction. And for the next hour we went at it. But this conversation was markedly different from all our other discussions over the past thirty years. The resistance my parents typically had was minimal this time, and when it surfaced, God gave me just the right words to diffuse it. It was probably as amazing an instance as any I have experienced of the Holy Spirit giving me the right words to say, in the right way, at the right time. My mom's Mormonism became a non-issue because I made it so; Christ and his gift of salvation was the issue. The same was true with my Dad's standard "What about people who have never heard of Christ?" type of questions. I addressed them in ways that seemed to satisfy him, again, by bringing the conversation back to the main issue.

The doctor arrived in the middle of our discussion, so I went out into the hall and prayed against the spiritual strongholds that were blinding the eyes of my parents. About a week previous to all this, God had shown my wife some new ways to pray for my folks. My spirit agreed with this, and we began to pray accordingly. I don't think it was a mere coincidence that my parents became so open to the gospel a week after we started praying that way! Of course, it didn't hurt that I had a "captive audience" in the hospital room, with both of them in their mid-eighties, staring their own mortality and eternity right in the face.

Both my parents thought they were going to heaven, but their belief was really more of a wish than an assurance based on something concrete. When I pressed them for the reasons why they believed they were going to heaven and began to gently explain that their reasons were flawed, they were quite attentive. After the doctor left, I asked my parents if they would like to know for certain that they were going to heaven, if they would like to begin an eternal relationship with the God who created them for precisely that reason. They said they did! And so, in what was for me a surreal experience, I led them in a prayer of salvation. After over thirty years, God answered my prayers and saved my folks! I was beside myself with joy and thanksgiving. Visits with them in the ensuing days confirmed that their decisions were "legit."

Less than two weeks later, I got the call everyone with elderly parents dreads: Dad had collapsed on the floor at home, the paramedics were trying to revive him, and Mom was hysterical. I made it to the hospital just as they pronounced my hero dead.

During my years in ministry, I have seen "unreachable" kids radically transformed by Christ. I have seen many prodigals from my youth groups come back to the Lord after decades of rebellion. I have volumes of journals that record God's answers to my prayers and the prayers of my youth staff teams. But there is nothing like this series of events surrounding my parents' salvation to remind me that "the Lord is not slow in keeping his promise, as some understand slowness. He is patient with you, not wanting anyone to perish, but everyone to come to repentance" (2 Peter 3:9).

Patient, expected hope was rewarded in the case of my dad and mom. Patient, expectant hope will be rewarded, youth worker, if you do not "grow weary and lose heart" (Hebrews 12:3). Thirty-year prayers *will* be answered. The seeds you sow in the lives of your students *will* bear fruit in due time. Today's hopeless students *will* become tomorrow's spiritual leaders.

The symphony is not over. The orchestra still must play. Don't give up.

FINALE

FOR AN
AUDIENCE OF ONE
The Heart of Youth Ministry

---

au•di•ence (ô′dē-əns)

1. The spectators or listeners assembled at a performance.
2. A body of adherents; a following.
3. The act of hearing or attending.

I've always been a "Trekkie." I got hooked on the original *Star Trek* series back in the '60s and was one of the first at the theater door when the Star Trek movies hit the big screen. As a teenager I never tired of hearing that classic introduction, "Space: the final frontier. These are the voyages of the Starship Enterprise. Its five-year mission . . . " and so on. The closing line was the clincher: "To boldly go where no man has gone before." It still gives me **goose bumps.***

*I GET GOOSE BUMPS A LOT.

As excited as I get over Star Trek though, the possibility of reaching new frontiers in ministry excites me even more. According to Dann Spader, a student of the history of revival, we are living in a time ripe for a large spiritual revival.

■   ■   ■

Many today sense we are on the verge of a great spiritual awakening. J. Edwin Orr, acknowledged authority on revivals, said, "Spiritual awakening does not come like a lightening bolt out of the blue—normally a decade or so of preparation precedes a major national revival." Recently, David Mains cited six signs in the church today as evidence that we are in just such a prelude period: a deep desire for worship; a growing commitment to prayer; strong preaching; a resurgence of service ministries; personal rededication preceding public outreach; a high level of commitment among young people.

Note that final sign carefully. Are we on the verge of another awakening? And if so, what role might our young people have in it? Perhaps a backward glance at America's awakenings and revivals will give an insight into what we might expect.

The first Great Awakening occurred in America in the late 1730's-40's. It was preceded by the preaching of Samuel Stoddard, a puritan pastor who for many years insisted that spiritual awakening was the only answer to the problems of his day. His preaching impacted his young grandson, Jonathan Edwards. At 17, Edwards graduated from Yale and became the pastor of the Northampton Congregational Church. In 1734-35, Jonathan Edwards became one of the three leaders of this first Great Awakening. His "Sinners in the Hands of an Angry God" is still read today.

The second Great Awakening lasted from the mid 1790's until 1840. It changed the moral fiber of this country. In the middle colonies, a teenager named Francis Asbury came to Christ and began preaching across the country. Self-disciplined, he preached over 16,000 sermons, ordained 4,000 preachers, and traveled 270,000 miles on horseback, wearing out 6 horses in the process.

Out of this second Great Awakening came the Young People's Missionary Societies, the Sunday School movement; and the Student Volunteer Movement which eventually sent 40,000 young adults into worldwide missions in "The Great Century of Christian Advancement." Eight major benevolent organizations started during this period; their combined budgets were the equivalent of $175,000,000, which equaled the Federal Budget of the time.

The third Great Awakening in America, from 1857-59, was for the most part a lay-led movement of prayer. At the time the nation was divided, heading toward civil war. On September 23, 1857, Jeremiah Lanphier, at the urging of a YMCA member, gave a public invitation for prayer. Six came the first week, followed by 20, then 40, then it went to daily meetings. In 6 months there were 10,000 gathering daily in New York and from there it spread across the country. Orr wrote, "The influence of the awakening was felt everywhere in the nation. It affected all classes. The number of conversions reported soon reached 50,000 weekly. Within two years, a million converts had been added to the churches of America."

The fourth Great Awakening was global. Commonly called the "Welch Revival," it occurred during 1904-05. Prior to this awakening, Francis Clark challenged his youth group to spiritual growth and accountability. That group became "Christian Endeavor," forerunner to today's youth ministries. In 14 years there were 40,000 "Endeavor Clubs" involving 2,000,000 young people in dedicated prayer. At that time, Seth Joshua, an evangelist in Wales, was so concerned about the condition in churches, he took a leave to pray that God would "raise up a lad from the coal mines or fields of Wales to revive His work." Two years later a young man "from the fields," Evan Roberts, was raised up by God. He told his friends, "I have a vision of all Wales being lifted up to heaven. We are going to see the mightiest revival that Wales has ever seen. I believe God is going to draw 100,000 souls to Himself." Within a year, 100,000 had come to Christ. . . . Businesses prospered as people paid back what they had stolen. And this revival spread around the world and strongly impacted churches in America. There is no doubt that young people were the catalyst to this awakening.

Since that time there have been periodic moments of revival, but nothing like the great awakenings of the past. Around and after World War II, Youth for Christ, Young Life, Word of Life, and similar ministries began. During this period of youth ministry expansion, rallies filled Madison Square Garden and Carnegie Hall. Four thousand gathered in Philadelphia, 5,000 in Boston, and 65,000 at Soldier Field in Chicago. Revivals broke out on many college campuses. Even at the high school level there were thousands of people coming to Christ. New student ministries flourished like Campus Crusade, Fellowship of Christian Athletes, InterVarsity Christian Fellowship, Basic Youth Conflicts, and youth clubs like AWANA, Boys Brigade and Pioneer Girls.

How is this significant for today? History has shown that before any great spiritual awakening there is a period of preparation marked by increased prayer and a growing commitment to evangelism—especially among the young people of that generation. For example, ten to twelve years before the "Welch Revival" broke out, over

2 million young people, under the banner of Christian Endeavor, were praying for revival. Today we see something quite similar: See You at the Pole has far surpassed that 2 million number, and that once-a-year "moment" is being turned into a "movement" as the growing number of student concerts of prayer and city-wide prayer rallies are being joined by the burgeoning number of student-led, prayer-oriented campus clubs.

I personally believe we are on the edge of the greatest awakening and spiritual harvest of all mankind—what an exciting day to be alive![1]

■   ■   ■

When I read Spader's comments, taken in the context of what we have covered in the previous pages, I get fired up. The "greatest awakening and spiritual harvest of all mankind" is certainly "where no man has gone before," and there is a holy adventurousness inside me that **squirms with anticipation,*** just as I used to squirm in that theater seat waiting for Kirk, Spock and the gang to do their galactic gig.

Spader's analysis is supported by a growing number of reports and stories from around the country (and the world) indicating that we may be getting very close to that

*THIS IS A MUCH BETTER SQUIRM.

"edge" of awakening. While it may be tempting to question the accuracy of these reports, the mere weight of evidence that continues to emerge is more than enough to persuade any doubting Thomas (or Mike) that unprecedented spiritual awakening is imminent, and in many places is already emerging.

Will youth ministry be a part of this national and global awakening? Will Spader's comments become prophetic? Will youth workers and students be at the forefront of renewal and awakening in our land? Will we see God change the destiny of generations of youth? Will youth ministry (and youth workers) get turned inside out? We still have **a long way to go,*** but I'm optimistic that we can get headed in the right direction and see a harvest among youth that will blow our doors off!

*THAT'S WHY I WROTE THIS BOOK.

However, we must remember that our ultimate goal is *not* to seek renewal or revival or the fulfillment of the Great Commission, as noble as those goals are; rather, our goal is to seek the Lord Jesus Christ, to love him, follow him and obey him. Francis Frangipane comments:

> My personal attitude is this: I will stand for revival, unity, and prayer. I will labor to restore healing and reconciliation between God's people. Yet, if all God truly wanted was to raise up one fully yielded son, a son who would refuse to be offended, refuse to react, refuse to harbor unforgiveness regardless of those who slander and persecute—I have determined to be that person. My primary goal in all things is not revival, but to bring pleasure to Christ.
>
> . . . In our immaturity, we have sought to be known for many things. We sought to make a name for ourselves through our spiritual gifts or doctrinal emphasis. Some sought renown for their type of church government; others desired recognition through a building or evangelistic program.

Today, if we seek renown it must be for this alone: to be known for knowing Christ. His promise is that His Presence—His very Spirit and power—will uninhibitedly accompany those who follow only Him. Thus, our focus must be upon Christ alone, for through Him God will ultimately accompany our lives with great glory. Yes, great signs and wonders will increasingly flow from our hands, but the miraculous will not distract our gaze from Jesus. For we are not seeking the *power* of God, but the *person* of God. When our hands are not being laid upon the sick, they will be lifted up in worship.[2]

May renewed youth workers throughout the United States, as well as around the world, be among those mentioned by the prophet Zechariah:

This is what the LORD Almighty says: "Many peoples and the inhabitants of many cities will yet come, and the inhabitants of one city will go to another and say, 'Let us go at once to entreat the LORD and seek the LORD Almighty. I myself am going.'" (Zechariah 8:20-21)

You see, when all is said and done, our symphony of youth ministry, played, as it were, from the inside out on both a personal and corporate level, is all for the honor and glory and praise of an audience of One.

THIRTEEN

COURAGEOUS
FAITH

The Risk of Inside-Out Youth
Ministry

---

cour•age (kûr′ĭj)

The state or quality of mind or spirit that enables one to face
danger, fear and/or challenges with self-possession, confidence and resolution; bravery.

I have never been scuba diving. My bride, Terri, is certified in
it, but I've never gotten around to going through the course. So
we settle for snorkeling if we are in an appropriate locale. It's
not as exciting as scuba diving, but it does have its moments,
especially in the ocean where there is stuff worth seeing.

The Oregon coast is not exactly a prime snorkeling spot; the
water is usually murky, and your
head turns blue from the cold, which
makes it hard to get the mask sealed
on your face—at least for me. (Having
a mustache doesn't help with the **seal
issue.**)* But on occasion we get to visit
places where the water is warmer, vis-
ibility is good, and the stuff we see is
pretty cool. We have tried to introduce
our children Lilly and Levi to snorkel-
ing; they have given it a try with a bit of success, but are a little

**✱NOR DOES
HAVING
A RATHER, UM,
LARGER THAN
AVERAGE
CRANIUM.**

reluctant to stick their heads underwater and trust the snorkel. I imagine sticking one's head dozens of feet underwater and trusting the scuba air tank would make one even more reluctant.

I don't think scuba had been **invented*** when the Israelites were preparing to enter the Promised Land after a forty-year camping trip. But as that gigantic camping party waited on the banks of the Jordan River, I bet there were more than a few nervous people in the group. Only Joshua and Caleb had been around when Moses led them across the Red Sea. Not only were the Israelites concerned about conquering people who had been described by the first team of scouts (Joshua and Caleb being the dissenters) as of great size and as very powerful (Numbers 13:26-33); they were also wondering how they were going to get across the Jordan River at flood stage.

*IF SCUBA HAD BEEN INVENTED, A FEW EGYPTIANS MIGHT HAVE SURVIVED THE RED SEA.

The fact that they were afraid did not catch God by surprise, which is why he told Joshua repeatedly to "be strong and courageous." And it is why Joshua instructed his officers to give the following orders to the people: "When you see the ark of the covenant of the LORD your God, and the priests, who are Levites, carrying it, you are to move out from your positions and follow it. Then you will know which way to go, *since you have never been this way before*" (Joshua 3:3-4, italics mine).

I am involved in a city-reaching youth ministry movement called the Joshua Revolution. We plan our events during "power sessions" with students; I sit next to the program director to offer input from the prayer team. It's a great fit and a thoroughly enjoyable experience for me. There are times when we sense that God is leading us away from our scripts, however, and asking us to trust him in new ways. While planning a recent conference with the theme "River of God" (from Ezekiel 47), a coworker and I started referring to these leadings from God as "snorkeling": jumping into the River and letting the current carry us along, even when sometimes we wind up under water.

Such an experience can be scary, but I'm learning to enjoy it more and more. And I'm growing less reluctant to snorkel, instead following the counsel of Proverbs 3:5-6:

> Trust in the LORD with all your heart
> and lean not on your own understanding;
> in all your ways acknowledge him,
> and he will make your paths straight.

*THAT'S A BIG IF. "Snorkeling" during Joshua Revolution events doesn't mean shabby preparation or irresponsible leadership; we have a pretty good idea of what makes for an effective youth ministry event. Rather, it means trusting the Lord when the Spirit prompts us to lean not on our own understanding. God has a much better idea of how to connect students to him, and he will tell us **if*** we are listening.

Sometimes I get criticized when I jump in the River. I understand the criticism; I've done a lot of whitewater rafting, and I know enough about the dangers to be enraged when my students jump out of the raft. But when I'm prompted by the Spirit to jump in the river, I try not to let criticism dissuade me. I am growing increasingly comfortable with spiritual snorkeling—I'm about ready to break out the scuba gear and go way under!

I hope you are too. For many, some aspects of inside-out

youth ministry are new, and to implement them will require courageous faith. But God is faithful, and if we entrust our ways to his purposes, he will make our paths straight.

Jump on in!

SELAH

*Of the Father's love begotten, ere the worlds began to
    be,*

He is Alpha and Omega, He the source, the ending He,

*Of the things that are and have been, and that future
    years shall see,*

Evermore and evermore!

*O ye heights of heaven, adore Him; angel hosts, His
    praises sing;*

*Powers, dominions, bow before Him, and extol our
    God and King.*

*Let no tongue on earth be silent, every voice in concert
    ring,*

Evermore and evermore!

*Christ, to Thee, with God the Father, and O Holy Ghost,
    to Thee,*

*Hymn and chant and high thanksgiving, and
    unwearied praises be;*

Honor, glory, and dominion, and eternal victory,

Evermore and evermore!

"OF THE FATHER'S LOVE BEGOTTEN"
AURELIUS CLEMENS PRUDENTIUS (A.D. 348-413)

Notes

Prelude: The Youth Ministry Symphony
[1]All definitions are adapted from *The American Heritage Electronic Dictionary* © 1992 Houghton Mifflin.
[2]George Barna, *Third Millennium Teens* (Ventura, Calif.: Barna Research Group, 1999), pp. 66-67.

Chapter 1: "I Am Desperate"
[1]Leonard Sweet, *SoulTsunami* (Grand Rapids, Mich.: Zondervan, 1999), p. 165.
[2]Mark Senter, *The Coming Revolution in Youth Ministry* (Wheaton, Ill.: Victor, 1992), pp. 29, 16.
[3]Nancy Leigh DeMoss, "Revival in the Heart: Choosing Brokenness," Revive Our Hearts, <www.ReviveOurHearts.com>.
[4]Tim St. Clair, "The Heart That God Revives," in *Herald of His Coming* (November 1998).

Chapter 2: "I Am Ruined"
[1]J. D. Douglas and Merrill C. Tenney, *The NIV Compact Dictionary of the Bible* (Grand Rapids, Mich.: Zondervan, 2000). Software edition used in OakTree Software's Accordance 4.3.
[2]Joe Aldrich, *Reunitis* (Sisters, Ore.: Questar, 1994), p. 119.
[3]Dave Busby, personal correspondence with the author from 1995, quoted in Mike Higgs, *Preparing Youth Ministry for the Coming Revival* (San Diego: National Network of Youth Ministries, 1996), p. 34.
[4]Ibid., pp. 35-36.
[5]Billy Graham, *Just As I Am* (New York: HarperCollins, 1998), pp. 823-44.
[6]Tom Phillips, *Revival Signs* (Gresham, Ore.: Vision House, 1995), p. 245.

Chapter 3: "I Am Wounded"
[1]David Roper, *A Burden Shared* (Grand Rapids, Mich.: Discovery House, 1991), pp. 12-13.
[2]Ibid., p. 12.

[3]Henri J. M. Nouwen, *The Wounded Healer* (New York: Doubleday, 1972), pp. 82-83.

Interlude: A Gift of Mercy
[1]Mary Rose O'Reilley, quoted in a promotional mailing for *Weavings: A Journal of the Christian Spiritual Life*.

Chapter 4: "I Am Safe"
[1]David Wilcox, "Eye of the Hurricane," from the album *How Did You Find Me Here?* (A&M Records, 1989).
[2]Francis Frangipane, *The Stronghold of God* (Orlando: Creation House, 1998), pp. vii-viii.

Chapter 6: "I Am Here"
[1]From the classic TV cartoon *The Jetsons*.
[2]Francis Frangipane, *The Stronghold of God* (Orlando: Creation House, 1998), pp. 14-15.

Chapter 7: "I Am a Warrior"
[1]John Dawson, *Healing America's Wounds* (Ventura, Calif.: Gospel Light, 1994), pp. 78, 98.
[2]Lance Lambert, *Spiritual Protection* (Kent, U.K.: Sovereign World Limited, 1991), p. 5.
[3]Ibid., p. 12.
[4]Peter Wagner, *Engaging the Enemy* (Ventura, Calif.: Gospel Light, 1991), pp. 7-8.

Chapter 8: "I Am Not Alone"
[1]Peter Wagner, *Prayer Shield* (Ventura, Calif.: Gospel Light, 1992), p. 19.
[2]Bo Boshears with Kim Anderson, *Student Ministry for the 21st Century* (Grand Rapids, Mich.: Zondervan, 1997), p. 51.
[3]Wagner, *Prayer Shield*, pp. 122-24.
[4]Alice Smith and Eddie Smith, *Spiritual Housecleaning* (Ventura, Calif.: Regal, 2003).
[5]Chuck D. Pierce and Rebecca Wagner Sytsema, *Ridding Your Home of Spiritual Darkness* (Colorado Springs: Wagner Institute For Practical Ministry, 1999), p. 17.

Chapter 9: "We Are One"
[1]Chuck Colson with Ellen Santilli Vaughn, *The Body: Being Light in Darkness* (Dallas: Word, 1992), p. 103.

[2] Joe Aldrich, *Reunitis* (Sisters, Ore.: Questar Publishers, 1994), p. 64.

[3] Cindy Jacobs, *The Voice of God* (Ventura, Calif.: Gospel Light, 1995), pp. 240-41.

[4] John Dawson, *Healing America's Wounds* (Ventura, Calif.: Gospel Light, 1994), p. 89.

[5] Pastors prayer summits, as defined and facilitated by International Renewal Ministries, are usually three and a half days long; the youth worker prayer gatherings that I facilitate through IRM are often shorter in duration, so I choose to call them retreats to avoid confusion and maintain the summit distinctive.

[6] Quoted in Tom Phillips, *Revival Signs* (Gresham, Ore.: Vision House, 1995), p. 157.

Chapter 10: "We Are Asking"

[1] Dick Eastman, *The Hour That Changes the World* (Grand Rapids, Mich.: Baker, 1978), p. 16.

[2] Steve Hawthorne and Graham Kendrick, *Prayerwalking* (Orlando: Creation House, 1993), p. 10.

Chapter 11: "We Are Listening"

[1] From the chapter titles of Gordon Aeschliman's *Global Trends: Ten Changes Affecting Christians Everywhere* (Downers Grove, Ill.: InterVarsity Press, 1990).

[2] From the chapter titles of Robert Stearns' *Prepare the Way: Twelve Spiritual Signposts for the New Millennium* (Lake Mary, Fla.: Creation House).

[3] From chapter 3 of Mike Higgs, *Preparing Youth Ministry for the Coming Revival* (San Diego: National Network of Youth Ministries, 1996).

[4] George Otis, *The Last of the Giants* (Tarrytown, N.Y.: Chosen, 1991), p. 85.

[5] Some of these books include Peter Wagner's *Breaking Strongholds in Your City* (Ventura, Calif.: Regal, 1993), and George Otis, *Informed Intercession* (Ventura, Calif.: Gospel Light, 1999).

[6] Ed Silvoso, *That None Should Perish* (Ventura, Calif.: Gospel Light, 1994), p. 154.

[7] Tom White, *Breaking Strongholds* (Ann Arbor, Mich.: Vine , 1993), p. 14.

Chapter 12: For an Audience of One

[1] Dann Spader, personal correspondence from 1995, quoted in Mike Higgs, *Preparing Youth Ministry for the Coming Revival* (San Diego: National Network of Youth Ministries, 1996), pp. 81-85.

[2] Francis Frangipane, *The Stronghold of God* (Lake Mary, Fla.: Creation House, 1998), pp. 112-13, 128-29.